MAY 1997

PEOPLES OF EAST AFRICA

THE DIAGRAM GROUP

Facts On File, Inc.

Peoples of Africa: Peoples of East Africa

Diagram Visual Information Ltd

Editorial director:	Bridget Giles
Contributors:	Trevor Day, Theodore Rowland Entwistle, David Lambert, Keith Lye, Oliver Marshall, Christopher Priest
Editors:	Margaret Doyle, Moira Johnston, Ian Wood
Indexer:	David Harding
Art director/designer:	Philip Patenall
Artists:	Chris Allcott, Darren Bennett, Bob Garwood, Elsa Godfrey, Brian Hewson, Kyri Kyriacou, Janos Marffy, Kathy McDougall, Patrick Mulrey, Rob Shone, Graham Rosewarne, Peter Ross
Production director:	Richard Hummerstone
Production:	Mark Carry, Lee Lawrence, Ollie Madden, Philip Richardson, Dave Wilson
Research director:	Matt Smout
Researchers:	Pamela Kea, Chris Owens, Catherine Michard, Neil McKenna

With the assistance of:

Dr Elizabeth Dunstan, International African Institute, School of Oriental and African Studies, University of London

David Hall, African studies bibliographer at the School of Oriental and African Studies, University of London

Horniman Museum, London

Museum of Mankind library, British Museum

Survival International

WWF-UK

Facts On File Inc.
11 Penn Plaza
New York NY 10001

Library of Congress Cataloging-in-Publication Data

Peoples of East Africa / the Diagram Group.
    p.   cm. – (Peoples of Africa)
    Includes index.
    ISBN 0-8160-3484-2 (alk. paper)
    1. Ethnology–Africa, Eastern. 2. Africa, Eastern–Social life
and customs. I. Diagram Group. II. Series: Peoples of Africa (New
York, N.Y.)
GN658.P46 1997
305. 8'009676–dc20   96-38735

Facts On File books are available at special discounts when purchased in bulk quantities for businesses, associations, institutions, or sales promotions. Please call our Special Sales Department in New York at 212/967-8800 or 800/322-8755.

Cover design by Molly Heron

Printed in the United States of America

RRD DIAG 10 9 8 7 6 5 4 3 2 1

This book is printed on acid-free paper

Contents

Foreword   4–5

THE REGION

East Africa today   6–7
Land   8–9
Climate   10–11
Vegetation   12–13
Wildlife   14–15
Chronology   16–21
Pictorial history   22–23
Distribution of peoples   24–25

THE PEOPLES

Peoples pages are in bold; special features are in italics
Introduction   26–31
Afar   32–35
East Africa: the birthplace of humanity   36–37
Amhara   38–41
The early Christian Church in Ethiopia   42–43
East African Asians   44–47
Falasha   48–51
Ganda   52–55
Coffee, tea, and other cash crops   56–57
Hutu and Tutsi   58–61
Karamojong   62–65
Kikuyu   66–69
Maasai   70–75
How tourism affects the people of East Africa   76–79
Nyamwezi   80–83
Nyoro   84–87
Oromo   88–91
Hairstyles: the practical and the fantastic   92–93
Somalis   94–97
Swahili   98–103

Appendix: East African languages   104–105
Glossary   106–109
Index   110–112

Foreword

Peoples of East Africa, the third volume in the Facts On File *Peoples of Africa* series, focuses on the historical and cultural richness of the east of the continent. This area covers the nations of Burundi, Djibouti, Eritrea, Ethiopia, Kenya, Malawi, Rwanda, Somalia, Tanzania, and Uganda. The island nation of Seychelles, off the east coast, is also part of this region. *Inside this volume the reader will find:*

- **The region:** preliminary pages describing in depth the region – its land, climate, vegetation, and wildlife – and others providing a broad historical overview and a current political profile of East Africa as a whole.
- **The people:** profiles of fifteen major ethnic groups within East Africa, describing the **history, language, ways of life, social structure,** and **culture and religion** of each group. A map has been included for each ethnic group to show the general region a group inhabits or is most concentrated in. The people profiles are arranged alphabetically. They are not intended to be encyclopedic; instead, they highlight particular aspects of a culture, focusing on fascinating details that will remain with the reader.
- **Special features:** tinted pages interspersed throughout the volume, each on a particular topical or cultural subject. Historical theme spreads, such as that on early humans, describe findings that suggest that this region of Africa was the cradle of many aspects of human civilization. Other features, such as that on cash crops, illustrate the way a country's economic constraints affect the lifestyles of its citizens. Another feature illustrates the great variety to be found in cultural aspects such as hairstyles.
- **Language appendix:** a diagrammatic outline of the African language families, which can be used to locate the languages of the peoples profiled and to see how they relate to other African languages.
- **Glossary and index:** following the profiles, features, and appendix are a comprehensive glossary defining the unfamiliar terms used within the volume and a complete index to the volume. Words that appear in the glossary have been printed in roman in special features and *italics* elsewhere.

Taken as a whole, *Peoples of East Africa* is intended to project a living portrait of the region that, with the other volumes in the series, provides the reader with a memorable snapshot of Africa as a place of rich heritage, far-reaching influence, and ongoing cultural diversity.

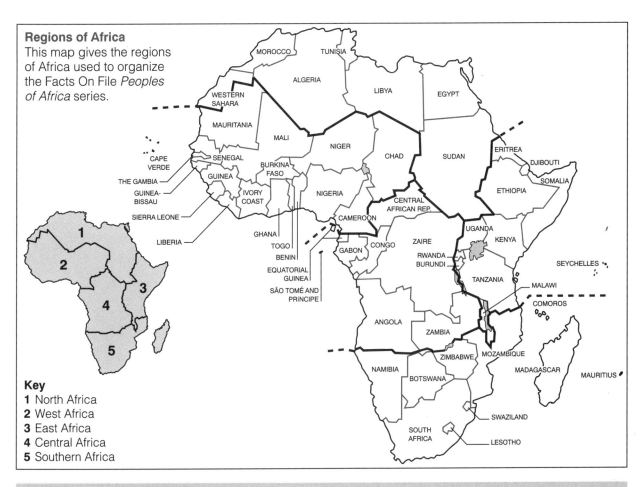

Regions of Africa

This map gives the regions of Africa used to organize the Facts On File *Peoples of Africa* series.

MOROCCO
TUNISIA
ALGERIA
WESTERN SAHARA
LIBYA
EGYPT
MAURITANIA
MALI
NIGER
CHAD
SUDAN
ERITREA
DJIBOUTI
CAPE VERDE
SENEGAL
BURKINA FASO
THE GAMBIA
GUINEA
GUINEA-BISSAU
SIERRA LEONE
IVORY COAST
NIGERIA
CENTRAL AFRICAN REP.
ETHIOPIA
SOMALIA
LIBERIA
GHANA
TOGO
BENIN
EQUATORIAL GUINEA
SÃO TOMÉ AND PRÍNCIPE
CAMEROON
GABON
CONGO
ZAIRE
RWANDA
BURUNDI
UGANDA
KENYA
SEYCHELLES
TANZANIA
MALAWI
COMOROS
ANGOLA
ZAMBIA
MOZAMBIQUE
ZIMBABWE
MADAGASCAR
MAURITIUS
NAMIBIA
BOTSWANA
SWAZILAND
SOUTH AFRICA
LESOTHO

Key
1 North Africa
2 West Africa
3 East Africa
4 Central Africa
5 Southern Africa

A word about ethnic groups

The series *Peoples of Africa* focuses on ethnic groups or peoples, useful but difficult-to-define terms. In the past, the word "tribe" was used to describe ethnic groupings, but this is today considered an offensive and arbitrary label. It is incorrect to refer to a group of people who may number in the hundreds of thousands and who have a long history of nation building as a tribe. "Tribe" is now generally used only to describe a basic political unit that exists within some larger ethnic groups, not to describe the group itself. So what is an ethnic group? An ethnic group is distinct from race or nationality; the former is rarely used today because it requires broad and inaccurate generalizations; and the latter describes only the national boundaries within which a person is born or lives. Both categories are fraught with difficulty. For the purposes of this series, the term "ethnic group" is used to describe people who have a common language, history, religion, and cultural and artistic heritage; they may also have a common way of life and often live within the same geographical area.

There are probably more than a thousand ethnic groups in all of Africa. Many are related to one another, often in complex ways. Groups have subgroups and even sub-subgroups. Intermarriage, colonialism, conquest, and migration through the ages have led to many combinations and to an intermixing of influences. In our series we have chosen to focus on only a fraction of Africa's many ethnic groups. A number of factors – including population figures, available information, and recognition outside Africa – were used in making the selection. To a certain extent, however, it was an arbitrary choice, but one that we hope offers a vibrant picture of the people of this continent.

East Africa today

East Africa, the cradle of human evolution, is one of Africa's most majestic regions. It contains snowcapped mountains, huge lakes, and abundant, though threatened, wildlife, which is partly preserved in vast national parks. Economically, however, East Africa is the continent's poorest region. It lacks the mineral and fossil fuel reserves of other areas and its economic development has been hampered by many problems. About eighty-five percent of the people make their living by farming. The quality of life of most farmers is low because they live at subsistence level (producing only enough to provide the basic needs of their families). This precarious way of life collapses when natural disasters – especially prolonged *droughts* – ruin harvests, causing famine and suffering on a vast scale. Judged by their per capita (for each person) gross national products (GNPs), Rwanda, Eritrea, and Ethiopia, are the poorest countries, followed closely by Tanzania, Malawi, and Somalia. The economic growth of several countries has been put into reverse by civil war. Eritrea, which was united with Ethiopia in 1952, broke away in the early 1990s after a long and bitter war. Burundi and Rwanda have been rocked by appalling conflict between the Tutsi and the Hutu. Rival *clans* in Somalia have torn the country apart, effectively dividing it into three separate regions, while Uganda, following much bloody civil conflict, is still struggling to maintain national unity. Kenya is the most stable East African country. It has developed a strong tourist industry alongside its cash crop farming and a small but important manufacturing sector. Kenya has been held together by autocratic one-party rule and many of its leaders fear that a multiparty system could result in division and strife.

Major roads

Major railroads

Country	Population (1994: 000s)	Area (sq. mi)	Per capita GNP (1994: US$)
Burundi	6,200	10,747	160
Djibouti	603	8,958	780
Eritrea	3,482	45,405	115
Ethiopia	54,900	435,523	100
Kenya	26,000	224,961	250
Malawi	9,500	45,747	170
Rwanda	7,800	10,169	80
Seychelles	72	176	6,680
Somalia	8,775	246,201	150
Tanzania	28,800	364,900	140
Uganda	18,600	93,074	190

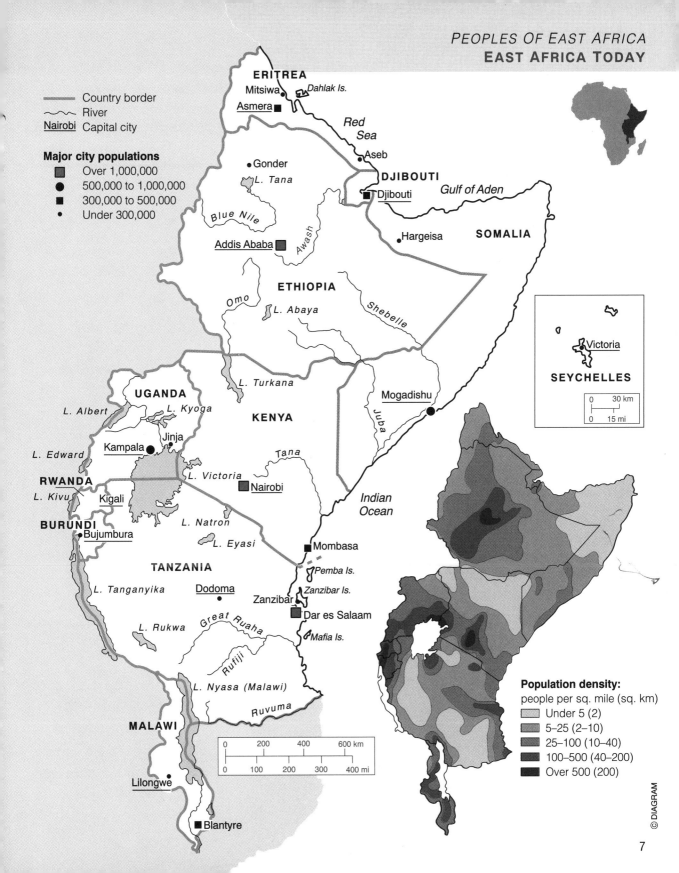

Major city populations
Country border
River
Nairobi Capital city

Over 1,000,000
500,000 to 1,000,000
300,000 to 500,000
Under 300,000

ERITREA
Mitsiwa
Dahlak Is.
Asmera
Red Sea
Aseb
Gonder
L. Tana
DJIBOUTI
Djibouti
Gulf of Aden
Blue Nile
Hargeisa
SOMALIA
Addis Ababa
Awash
ETHIOPIA
Omo
L. Abaya
Shebelle
L. Turkana
UGANDA
L. Albert
L. Kyoga
KENYA
Jinja
Juba
Kampala
Tana
Mogadishu
RWANDA
L. Edward
L. Victoria
Nairobi
Indian Ocean
L. Kivu
Kigali
BURUNDI
L. Natron
Bujumbura
L. Eyasi
Mombasa
TANZANIA
Pemba Is.
L. Tanganyika
Dodoma
Zanzibar Is.
Zanzibar
L. Rukwa
Great Ruaha
Dar es Salaam
Mafia Is.
Rufiji
L. Nyasa (Malawi)
Ruvuma
MALAWI
Lilongwe
Blantyre

Victoria
SEYCHELLES
| 0 | 30 km |
| 0 | 15 mi |

| 0 | 200 | 400 | 600 km |
| 0 | 100 | 200 | 300 | 400 mi |

Population density:
people per sq. mile (sq. km)
Under 5 (2)
5–25 (2–10)
25–100 (10–40)
100–500 (40–200)
Over 500 (200)

© DIAGRAM

7

Land

East Africa is bordered on the north by the Red Sea and the Gulf of Aden and on the east by the Indian Ocean. It is Africa's most mountainous area as it contains most of the Great Rift Valley – a depression that extends from the Jordan River Valley in southwest Asia right across East Africa. Much of the region consists of plateaus, in places overlooked by snowcapped peaks, and gashed by steep troughs hundreds of miles long. East Africa has the continent's highest point – Mount Kilimanjaro at 19,340 ft (5,895 m) – and its lowest land: 509 ft (155 m)

Rift Valley system

Formed in prehistoric times by shifting land masses, the Great Rift Valley cuts through East Africa in two main sections. The Eastern Rift system runs from the Red Sea through Ethiopia, Kenya, and Tanzania and contains the Ethiopian Highlands. The Western Rift system runs down the west of Uganda, Rwanda, Burundi, and Tanzania and then through Malawi. The Great Rift Valley is actually a series of valleys each of which can be up to 34 miles (54 km) across. The steep valley sides descend to floors formed by slabs of the Earth's crust that slipped down between the flanking highlands. The deepest troughs contain long, narrow lakes – for example, Lake Tanganyika the world's longest freshwater lake. The next largest Rift Valley lakes are Nyasa (Malawi) and Turkana.

Eastern Highlands

The Eastern Highlands are grassy plains that provide grazing land for livestock and wildlife. These immense, open uplands occupy most of East Africa. They mostly lie 600–5,000 ft (200–1,500 m) above sea level but have vast stretches that are above 3,000 ft (900 m). In Somalia, the land rises in giant steps formed by escarpments (steep slopes or cliffs). Farther south, the Eastern Highlands occupy most of Tanzania and Uganda and nearly half of Kenya. The Eastern Rift of the Great Rift Valley splits the Eastern Highlands almost in two where it cuts through Tanzania and Kenya. The Eastern Highlands contain Lake Victoria, the world's second largest freshwater lake and the largest lake in Africa.

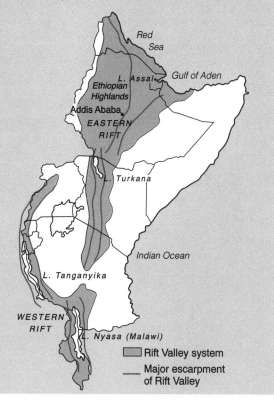

Rift Valley system

Major escarpment of Rift Valley

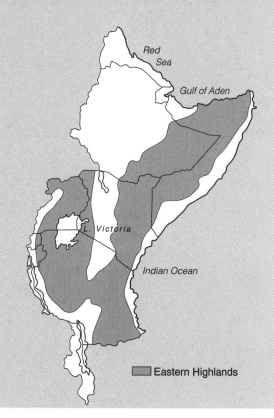

Eastern Highlands

below sea level at Lake Assal, Djibouti. Africa's highest city is the Ethiopian capital Addis Ababa, 8,000 ft (2,400 m) above sea level. From the lakes and rivers of East Africa rises the Nile, the world's longest river at 4,145 miles (6,671 km). Lakes Victoria, Albert, and Turkana are all sources of the Nile. The most densely populated areas of East Africa include much of Malawi, Rwanda, Burundi, Uganda, southern Kenya, and the Ethiopian Highlands.

Mountainous regions above 6,000 ft (1,800 m)

East Africa has a lot of land above 6,000 ft (1,800 m) and scores of peaks that are higher still. Almost all these mountains are volcanic, built by ash or lava escaping from cracks in the Earth's crust within the Great Rift Valley. Indeed, the majority of these mountains lie within the Rift system. The Ethiopian Highlands form the most extensive mountainous area, with vast rolling uplands 7,000–8,000 ft (2,100–2,400 m) high pierced by gorges and crowned by many peaks that are 10,000 ft (3,100 m) high or more. Farther south, several peaks exceed 10,000 ft (3,100 m) in the Ruwenzori Range – East Africa's only nonvolcanic mountains. Africa's tallest peak is the summit of Mount Kilimanjaro at 19,340 ft (5,895 m), which is a volcanic mountain in Tanzania.

Coastal lowlands

The coastline of East Africa makes a huge elbowlike shape formed by the Horn of Africa, which comprises Somalia and neighboring regions of Ethiopia and Djibouti. The northern shores are largely arid, but palm-lined sandy beaches fringe those that face the Indian Ocean. A very narrow belt of low land borders the Red Sea and Gulf of Aden where the mountains of the Great Rift Valley come down almost right next to the coast. The tip of the Horn of Africa is also mountainous. South of the Horn of Africa, a belt of coastal lowland faces the Indian Ocean to the east and is quite wide in parts. Offshore islands include Pemba and Zanzibar off the coast of Tanzania and Eritrea's Dahlak Islands. Coral reefs lie off the coasts of Kenya and Eritrea.

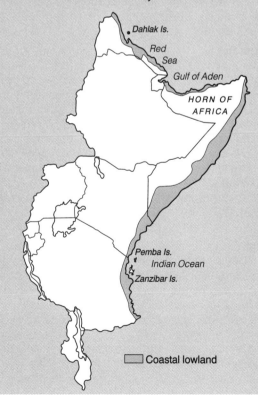

Land over 6,000 ft (1,800 m)

Coastal lowland

© DIAGRAM

Climate

East Africa has a variety of climates. Many areas have fairly constant daily temperatures, ranging from hot to cold depending largely on the altitude. The world's highest mean temperature measured over six years is 34 °C (94 °F) and was recorded at Dallol in the Danakil Desert of Ethiopia and Eritrea. At the equator, however, eternal snow crowns Mount Kenya, a peak 17,040 ft (5,198 m) high. The Horn of Africa (Somalia and neighboring parts of Ethiopia and Djibouti), the Red Sea coast, and northeast Kenya have an arid to semiarid climate – largely hot and dry, but with great swings in daily temperature. Apart from the highlands of Ethiopia and the Great Rift Valley, the rest of East Africa has a hot, tropical climate with both wet and dry seasons, though some western areas close to the equator receive several inches of rain every month. The highlands generally have cooler and wetter climates than elsewhere.

Winds

Between November and April, air pressure is lower over East Africa than over southwest Asia to the northeast. This pressure difference tends to draw northeast winds into East Africa from across the Red Sea and the Gulf of Aden. Farther south, northeast winds blow along East Africa's Indian Ocean coast and sometimes come in off the sea. Between May and October, air pressure is higher over East Africa than over southwest Asia but lower than over regions to the south, so air flows broadly north and northeast across the region. A southwesterly air flow reaches Ethiopia from Central Africa, while a southeasterly air flow from the Indian Ocean veers north to track up the East African coast.

Temperature

Temperature varies less with the seasons than with altitude. Coasts facing the Red Sea and Gulf of Aden are among the hottest places anywhere. Farther south, coastal plains near the equator are always warm. Mombasa on the Kenyan coast has an annual average temperature range of between 24 and 28 °C (76–82 °F). At 5,000 ft (1,500 m), Kenya's capital Nairobi is a pleasantly cool, 15 to 18 °C (59–65 °F). The Ethiopian Highlands enjoy refreshing springlike temperatures. At nights, however, upland temperatures can plunge by 14 °C (25 °F). Frosts frequently occur above 8,000 ft (2,400 m) and snow lies all the year round on many slopes above 14,000 ft (4,300 m).

Rainfall

Rainfall ranges from under 3 in. (8 cm) a year in the deserts of the Horn of Africa to more than 100 in. (254 cm) on some western volcanic mountains. Between May and October, moist air from the Indian Ocean brings heavy rainfall to the Ethiopian Highlands in the north. Meanwhile, dry air from the south moves over Malawi and southern Tanzania, so these get very little rain. Winds from the Indian Ocean bring some rain to the coast of Tanzania and Kenya but the Horn of Africa and the Red Sea coast stay mainly dry. Between November and April, dry air from southwest Asia keeps most of northern East Africa dry while moist breezes from the Indian Ocean bring rain to southern parts.

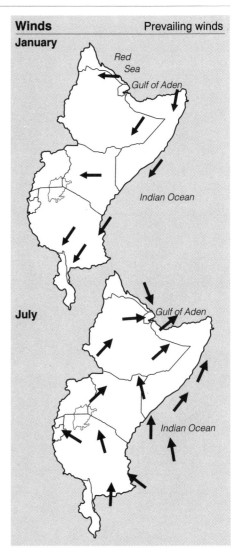

Winds Prevailing winds
January

Red Sea
Gulf of Aden
Indian Ocean

July

Gulf of Aden
Indian Ocean

Temperature

Actual surface temperature

January

July

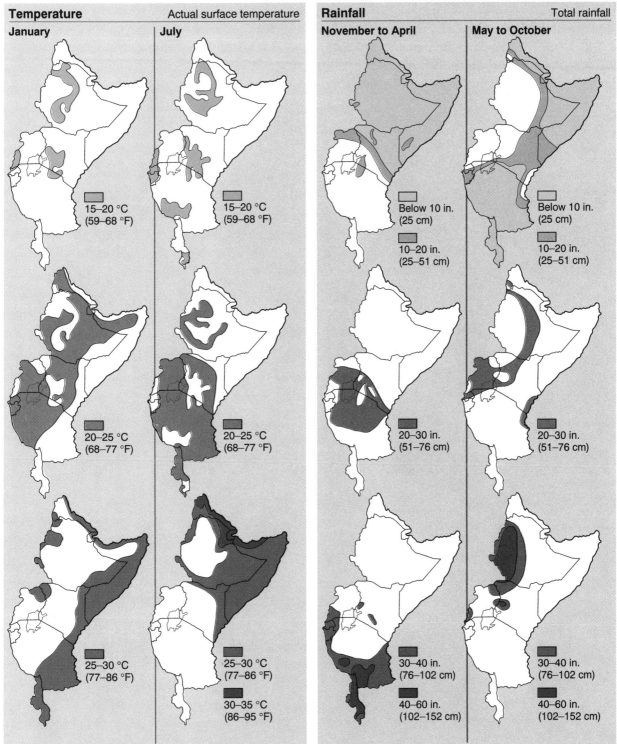

15–20 °C
(59–68 °F)

20–25 °C
(68–77 °F)

25–30 °C
(77–86 °F)

30–35 °C
(86–95 °F)

Rainfall

Total rainfall

November to April

May to October

Below 10 in.
(25 cm)

10–20 in.
(25–51 cm)

20–30 in.
(51–76 cm)

30–40 in.
(76–102 cm)

40–60 in.
(102–152 cm)

© DIAGRAM

Vegetation

Local differences in rainfall and altitude help create East Africa's wide variety of vegetation zones. Only *drought*-resistant plants survive in the deserts and semideserts of Ethiopia, Somalia, Eritrea, and northern Kenya. Tropical *savanna* (grassland with scattered trees and shrubs) covers the vast Eastern Highlands, but its character varies with rainfall. Forests clothe warm, moist valleys and the rainier lower slopes of mountains. Above the treeline comes

Desert and semidesert

East Africa has a few areas of desert, mainly around the Horn of Africa (Somalia and neighboring areas of Ethiopia and Djibouti). These regions have large stretches of bare ground with only a sparse scattering of plants. Small shrubs and low, thorny acacia trees put down deep roots to reach underground moisture. Leaves reduced to spines have small surface areas that limit the amount of water lost through evaporation. Some plants store water in underground bulbs. Small trees and shrubs such as the cactuslike euphorbias mark the course of dry river beds. Semidesert vegetation covers the majority of the region around the desert areas. Scattered tufts of grass; low, shrubby acacia trees; palm trees; and trees of the *Boswellia* genus, which yield the aromatic gum frankincense, grow in semidesert areas. In both desert and semidesert areas, the seeds of short, hard grasses can persist in the soil for years, sprouting quickly after rain to form short-lived pastures.

Typical plants
1 Doum palm
2 Date palm
3 Euphorbia

HORN OF AFRICA

▨ Desert and semidesert

Tropical savanna

The vegetation of tropical savanna regions varies according to rainfall. Regions with 12 to 20 in. (31–51 cm) of rainfall a year usually have a covering of thornbush. Plants include drought-resistant acacia trees, myrrh trees, and baobabs, which have thick trunks that can store large amounts of water. Dry region plants include the spider plant, often grown as a houseplant in the Northern Hemisphere. Regions with 20 to 30 in. (51–76 cm) of rain a year are covered by a sea of grasses that can be up to 4 ft (1.2 m) high. The grasses grow in clumps. Small shrubs and acacia trees rise above the grasses. Wooded savanna thrives near the equator where there is a dry season and the annual rainfall averages between 40 and 55 in. (102–140 cm). Grasses, such as elephant grass, grow more than head high among shrubs and trees that shed their leaves during droughts (water shortages generally caused by prolonged periods of inadequate rainfall).

Typical plants
1 Myrrh tree
2 Baobab
3 Spider plant

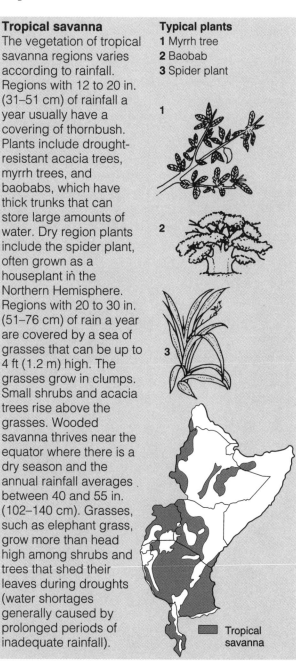

■ Tropical savanna

high-altitude, subalpine moorland and above that an alpine zone that has bizarre, giant relatives of some Northern Hemisphere garden plants. On land that is moist and level enough for farming, fields have now largely replaced the natural vegetation. Food crops include corn, cassava, beans, and wheat. Coffee, tea, tobacco, and *sisal* (a fiber crop) are the main crops sold for cash.

Tropical forest

On moist, lower slopes of the Western Rift are a few small areas of tropical *rainforest,* fragments of the dense forest that once stretched east from Central Africa to Lake Victoria. The majority of forests in East Africa are now tropical seasonal forests. In regions that have both wet and dry seasons, many of the trees are deciduous – they shed their leaves annually. Evergreens such as cedar, yellowwood, and camphor trees dominate the wetter slopes above 5,000 ft (1,500 m). Around 8,000 ft (2,400 m) these evergreens give way to a zone densely packed with mountain bamboo, which reaches up to 50 ft (15 m) high. In southwest Ethiopia, the lower highland slopes contain remnants of tropical forest, with large broadleaved trees hung with creepers and rising from a mass of ferns and shrubs including wild coffee bushes. Junipers monopolize the forest above. *Deforestation* (the clearing of forests) has severely affected many forests and few remain in Ethiopia today.

Typical plants
1 Wild coffee
2 Cedar
3 Mountain bamboo

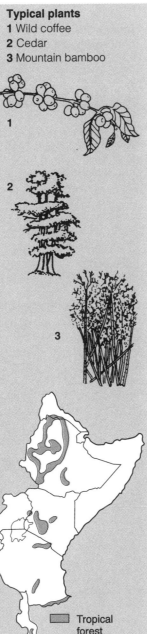

Tropical forest

Mountain

The highest mountain areas have cold-adapted plants that can survive the frost which forms each night as the thin air loses heat into the sky. Above 10,000 ft (3,100 m) occurs a subalpine moorland of coarse, tussock grasses, sedges (grasslike plants with narrow, pointed leaves and tiny flowers) and tree heaths (or brier, evergreen shrubs or trees with needlelike leaves) hung with lichens. Higher still stand treelike plants of the Afro-alpine zone – giant relatives of common lobelias and groundsels. Some species produce rosettes of leaves that sprout from pillarlike stems. The dead leaves stay on these plants, helping to insulate the stems against the intense cold that sets in after the Sun goes down. These oddities can grow up to 20 ft (6 m) high. Beneath them crouch mosses, small alpine grasses, and small, flowering plants of the *Helichrysum* genus. Flowering plants continue up to about 15,750 ft (4,800 m), but only lichens can endure the harsh cold of the highest summits.

Typical plants
1 Tree heath
2 Giant lobelia
3 Giant groundsel

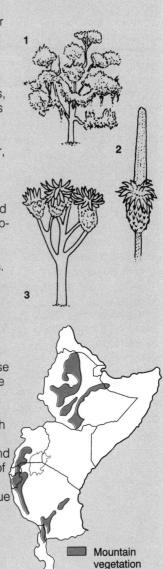

Mountain vegetation

© DIAGRAM

13

Wildlife

The wildlife of East Africa is among the most varied and splendid in the world. Tropical forest, tropical *savanna* (grasslands with scattered trees and shrubs), desert, mountain, river and lake, sea and seashore – each zone has its own set of mammals, birds, reptiles, and *invertebrates* (animals without backbones such as insects). The greatest wildlife spectacle of all occurs in the parklike grasslands. These are the only places on Earth where you can still see more than a million large, wild mammals roaming free. East Africa's big game shares the

Open countryside

East Africa's tropical savannas and semideserts house many spectacular animals. The Serengeti Plains of northern Tanzania, for example, teem with large grass-eating and tree-browsing mammals. Tourists can expect to see elephants, giraffes, rhinoceroses, zebras, and buffaloes. The many varieties of antelope include the large, cattlelike wildebeest (or gnu); the swift and graceful impala, which can jump as far as 30 ft (9 m); the oxlike eland (Africa's largest antelope); and the tiny dik dik. These herbivores (plant-eating animals) can coexist in the same area as they all live off different types of vegetation. Some of the larger herbivores become food for carnivores (meat-eaters). Chief among these are lions, leopards, cheetahs, and hyenas. Scavengers such as jackals and vultures can live off the remains of dead animals.

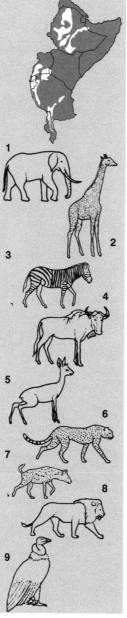

Typical animals
1 African elephant
2 Giraffe
3 Zebra
4 Wildebeest
5 Dik dik
6 Cheetah
7 Spotted hyena
8 Lion
9 Lappet-faced vulture

Mountain

Forests above 5,000 ft (1,500 m) have small species of buffalo and elephant, bongos (large, striped antelopes), tree hyraxes (small, rodentlike mammals), and galagos (nocturnal, tree-dwelling primates sometimes called bush babies). Forest hogs, bushbucks (small antelopes), and blue monkeys occupy the dense bamboo forests above 8,000 ft (2,400 m). Leopards hunt sure-footed klipspringer antelopes on rocky moors above 10,000 ft (3,000 m). Mice and rock hyraxes live with groove-toothed rats in the cold, alpine regions above the forests. Birds of the moorland and alpine zones include the lammergeier (a large, bearded vulture) and the tiny, brightly-colored malachite sunbird. Mountain mammals unique to Ethiopia include the simien fox (a jackal-like wolf), gelada (a baboon), and the mountain nyala (an antelope with large, spiral horns).

Typical animals
1 Leopard
2 Simien fox
3 Klipspringer
4 Mountain nyala
5 Gelada
6 Rock hyrax
7 Groove-toothed rat
8 Lammergeier
9 Malachite sunbird

land with a fast-multiplying human population though. To protect their wildlife, countries have set aside large tracts of land as game reserves and national parks. There are sixteen of these in Kenya alone. As the numbers of people grow, however, their need for food-producing land increases. In places, therefore, larger wild mammals such as lions, elephants, and certain antelopes are still being displaced or threatened by the demand for farming and grazing land.

River and lake

Large mammals found living in and around rivers and lakes include waterbucks (antelopes with long, forward-curving horns), hippopotamuses, sitatungas (antelopes whose splayed hooves help them travel on swampy ground), and marsh mongooses (short-legged, catlike mammals). Nile crocodiles, which are found throughout Africa, lie partly submerged in water to ambush their prey. Water birds include goliath herons, pelicans, and flamingoes. Hundreds of thousands of flamingoes feed in the soda-rich waters of some Rift Valley lakes. Rift Valley lakes are rich in fishes, especially cichlids (bony fishes), found nowhere else. Lake Nyasa (or Malawi) holds about 200 species of cichlid. African lungfishes and primitive, scaly fishes called bichirs, which can breathe air at times of need, also occur in some rivers and lakes.

Typical animals
1 Hippopotamus
2 Sitatunga
3 Marsh mongoose
4 Nile crocodile
5 Goliath heron
6 Greater flamingo
7 Lake Malawi cichlid
8 African lungfish
9 Bichir

Shore and sea

Along the Red Sea and Indian Ocean, muddy and rocky coasts are home to a great variety of animals. Muddy shores form winter feeding grounds for migrant curlews, sanderlings, and other wading birds. Mudskippers (fish that can leave the water to search for food) and crabs live in swamps. Offshore, sea turtles and the sea cows (sea-dwelling mammals) called dugongs browse on underwater meadows of seaweeds. Rocky coasts hold limpets, barnacles, and crabs that can survive great heat and dryness at low tide. Billions of tiny coral polyps build coral gardens where crabs, shrimps, clams, sea slugs, and starfish lurk. Above these coral reefs swim brightly-colored tropical fishes such as the clown fish, parrot fish, and the trigger fish. Some become food for large fishes, sharks, or people.

Typical animals
1 Dugong
2 Curlew
3 Sanderling
4 Green turtle
5 Mudskipper
6 Clown fish
7 Fiddler crab
8 Starfish
9 Sea slug

© DIAGRAM

Chronology

In the first millennium, early Axumite sculptors produce stone statues such as this one, probably for religious purposes.

During the golden age of Swahili culture (c. 1200–1500), metalworkers melt copper in clay pots such as these.

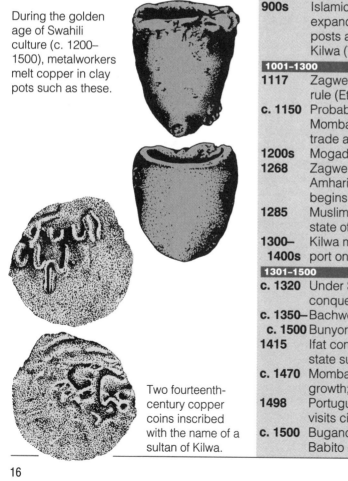

Two fourteenth-century copper coins inscribed with the name of a sultan of Kilwa.

EAST AFRICAN EVENTS	WORLD EVENTS
Countries or locations in parentheses give the modern day locations of the states. Dates of independence appear in a table after the chronology.	

to 1000 CE

1000 BCE	Cushitic peoples reach Kenyan Highlands after migrating from the Ethiopian Highlands	**c.1200 BCE** Beginning of Judaism
500 BCE –		**814** Carthage city-state founded
300 CE	Bantu-speaking people migrate into East Africa	**510** Republic of Rome established
200	Greek records mention Jews in Ethiopia	**c. 30 CE** Jesus of Nazareth crucified
c.100	Axumite Kingdom in Ethiopia	**455** Vandals sack Rome
300s	Axumites issue gold coinage	
320	Ezana first Christian king of Axum	**622** Muhammad's flight to Medina
324	Axumite Kingdom invades Meroitic Kingdom (Sudan)	**624** T'ang dynasty unites China
640 on	Rise of Islam; decline of Axumite Kingdom begins	
800s	Muslim Arabs settle Horn of Africa	**700s** Printing
900s	Islamic Somali nomads begin to expand southward; Arab trading posts at Mogadishu (Somalia) and Kilwa (Tanzania) established	begins to spread from China **793** Viking raids begin in Europe

1001–1300

1117	Zagwe dynasty begins rule (Ethiopia)	**1066** Normans conquer England
c. 1150	Probable founding date for both Mombasa and Malindi (Kenya) as trade and export centers on coast	**c. 1150** Angkor Wat built in Cambodia
1200s	Mogadishu the preeminent port	**c. 1200** Inca dynasty founded by
1268	Zagwe dynasty overthrown; Amharic Solomonic dynasty begins rule (Ethiopia)	Manco Capac **1206** Genghis Khan begins Mongol
1285	Muslim Afar unified under the state of Ifat; at war with Ethiopia	conquest of Asia **1237–41** Mongols
1300– 1400s	Kilwa most important trading port on east coast	overrun Eastern Europe

1301–1500

c. 1320	Under Sultan Sulaiman II, Kilwa conquers Mafia Islands (Zanzibar)	**1346–9** "Black Death" ravages
c. 1350– c. 1500	Bachwezi dynasty rules over Bunyoro-Kitara (Uganda)	much of Europe **1354** Moroccan explorer Ibn Battuta
1415	Ifat conquered by Ethiopia; Ifat state succeeded by Adal	begins his travels **1368** Ming dynasty
c. 1470	Mombasa begins period of growth; decline of Kilwa follows	begins in China
1498	Portuguese sailor Vasco da Gama visits cities on East African coast	**1492** Christopher Columbus
c. 1500	Buganda expands (Uganda); Babito rule over Bunyoro begins	discovers New World (Americas)

EAST AFRICAN EVENTS

1501–1700

1502–1509	Portuguese conquer East African coast to gain control of trade
1526	Adal declares a *jihad* (Islamic holy war) on Christian Ethiopia
1543	Ethiopia conquers Adal
c. 1550s	Bunyoro Kingdom at greatest extent. Tutsi people found kingdom of Ruanda (Rwanda)
1580	Portugal united with Spain
1600s	Tutsi kingdom in Urundi (Burundi)
1640	Portugal independent again
1652	Omani Arab traders begin to settle on East African coast
1699	Omanis control much of coast
1700s	Ethiopia splits into feudal states

1701–1850

1756	Seychelles made French territory
1794	Seychelles captured by British
1800s	Buganda supplants Bunyoro as most important regional kingdom
1814	Seychelles made British colony and base of antislavery patrols
1822–1837	East African coast under rule of Sultan of Oman
c. 1830	Babito prince of Bunyoro founds independent Toro Kingdom (Uganda)
1832	Zanzibar made capital of Oman
c. 1835	Slave caravans begin to visit interior of East Africa
c. 1840	Arrival of Ngoni, Bantu-speaking people from Southern Africa, fleeing Zulu attacks
1840s–1880s	Height of Swahili/Arab slave trade in East Africa
1850s	Oromo begin to establish Muslim kingdoms (southwest Ethiopia)

1851–1899

1859–1870	Bunyoro and Toro kingdoms at war
1855–1930	Series of attempts to resurrect Ethiopian Empire
1856	Zanzibar becomes an independent sultanate
1873	Zanzibar slave market closes
1884	French Somaliland (Djibouti) and British Somaliland (Somalia) established as colonies

WORLD EVENTS

1519–22	Magellan's world circumnavigation. Hernan Cortés conquers Aztecs
1526	Mughal Empire founded in India. Ottomans annex Hungary
1619	First African slaves arrive in Jamestown, Virginia
1620	*Mayflower* reaches New England, America
1776–83	American War of Independence
1789–99	French Revolution
1807	Britain outlaws slave trade
1815	Napoleon defeated at Waterloo
1816–28	Chile, Venezuala, Argentina, Brazil, Uruguay, and Peru gain independence
1823	Monroe Doctrine in US
1845–51	"Potato Famine" in Ireland
1846–8	US at war with Mexico
1853	US fleet forces Japan to open to US trade
1857–9	Indian Mutiny; India made British vice-royalty
1859	Charles Darwin publishes *The Origin of Species*

The Gereza (fortress) on Kilwa is built by the Portuguese in the sixteenth century. The Portuguese arrival on East Africa's Indian Ocean coast brings an end to the Swahili and Arab dominance of trade.

Sailing boats called *dhows* enable the Arabs to travel from southwest Asia, using the *monsoon* winds, to trade in East Africa and elsewhere. Some of these traders settle in the region as early as the tenth century.

The Zanzibar slave market in 1872. Although slavery is not new to the region, in the nineteenth century it reaches an unprecedented level.

© DIAGRAM

The 1896 Battle of Adowa (modern Adwa), in which the Ethiopian forces under Emperor Menelik II defeat the Italians.

During World War I in German East Africa, many Africans fight in the colonial armies. This Swahili scuplture portrays one of these "*askari*" soldiers.

This detention camp is set up at Nyeri, in Kenya, by the British in the 1950s and detains people suspected of involvement in the anticolonial Mau Mau uprising.

EAST AFRICAN EVENTS

1886	Anglo-German agreement defines European "spheres of influence" in East Africa and the boundaries of Sultanate of Zanzibar. Italian Somaliland (Somalia) established
1891	British declare a *protectorate* (colony) over Nyasaland (Malawi)
1895	British and Germans complete partition of Sultanate of Zanzibar. British take control of Kenya
1896	Italians defeated by Ethiopians at battle of Adowa; Ethiopia conquers Oromo kingdoms. Bunyoro and Toro kingdoms made British protectorates
1897	Urundi under German rule
1900	Buganda made a part of the British protectorate of Uganda

1901–1950

1914–1918	Many Africans fight in East Africa during WWI for Britain, Belgium, or Germany; colonies suffer and Germans lose territories
1916	Ruanda and Urundi occupied by Belgium
1930	Haile Selassie I becomes Emperor of Ethiopia
1935–1941	Italian forces invade and occupy Ethiopia
1939–1945	Many East Africans fight for Allies in India and Burma during WWII

1951–1970

1952	Eritrea federated to Ethiopia
1952–1956	Mau Mau rebellion in Kenya fights against British rule
1959	Hutu overthrow Tutsi monarchy in Ruanda
1961	Eritrean rebels begin armed struggle for independence
1963	Dr Hastings Banda becomes prime minister in Malawi
1964	Tanganyika and Zanzibar unite to form Tanzania
1965	Tutsi purge Hutu from army and bureaucracy in Rwanda
1966	Military coup in Burundi. Political coup in Uganda; prime minister Milton Obote becomes president

WORLD EVENTS

1861–5	US Civil War
1865	US abolishes slavery
1868	Meiji Restoration in Japan
1869	Suez Canal opened
1871	German Empire proclaimed
1875	Alexander Graham Bell invents the telephone
1898	Spanish-American War
1900	Antiforeigner Boxer Rebellion in China
1914–18	World War I (WWI)
1917	US enters WW1. Second Russian Revolution: socialism adopted
1930s	Worldwide depression
1939–45	World War II (WWII)
1946–7	Cold War begins
1952	First contraceptive pill ("The Pill") made
1955	Warsaw Pact signed by communist East Europe
1957	North and South Vietnam at war
1959	Cuban revolution led by Fidel Castro
1963	US President Kennedy is assassinated

EAST AFRICAN EVENTS

1967	Uganda abolishes traditional kingdoms. French Somaliland becomes the French Territory of the Afars and the Issas
1969	Peaceful coup in Somalia led by Maj. Gen. Muhammad Siad Barre

1971-1980

1971	Col. Idi Amin Dada seizes power in Uganda. Banda becomes president in Malawi
1972	Hutu people in Burundi revolt against Tutsi elite; civil war breaks out; over 100,000 Hutu killed. 80,000 Asians expelled from Uganda by Amin
1973	Military coup in Rwanda
1974	Haile Selassie I overthrown by army in Ethiopia; socialism adopted by military government
1976	Peaceful coup in Burundi
1977	Military coup in Seychelles. Maj. Mengistu Haile Mariam takes power in Ethiopia and launches "red terror" campaign. Conflict between Somalia and Ethiopia over Ogaden region
1978	Amin invades Tanzania
1979	Amin ousted by Ugandan and Tanzanian forces. Seychelles made a one-party state
1980s	Ethiopia and Somalia hold talks to end conflict over Ogaden region. Severe famine in Ethiopia

1981-1990

1981	Somali National Movement (SNM) begins guerilla activities. Djibouti becomes a one-party state. Failed coup attempt in Seychelles
1981–1986	Ugandan civil war; rebels led by Yoweri Museveni win power
1984–1985	"Operation Moses" 7,000 refugee Falasha airlifted from Sudan to Israel
1985	Military coup in Uganda
1986	Rebels oust military in Uganda
1987	Military coup in Burundi; clashes between Hutu and Tutsi. Ethiopian and Somalian forces clash. Failed coup in Seychelles

WORLD EVENTS

1969 Assassination of Dr Martin Luther King in Memphis, Tennessee. Neil Armstrong is first man on the Moon

1973 Oil Crisis and world recession after Arabs ban oil sales to US

1972 Direct UK rule in Northern Ireland

1974 "Watergate" scandal in US. Portuguese Revolution

1975 Communists reunite North and South Vietnam

1975–9 Khmer Rouge reign of terror in Cambodia

1978–9 Revolution in Iran

1979 Civil wars in Nicaragua and El Salvador

1979–89 Soviet troops in Afghanistan

1980–8 Iran-Iraq War: US backs Iraq

1982 Falklands War between UK and Argentina

1982–85 Israeli invasion of Lebanon

1986 Chernobyl nuclear accident in USSR

1989 Revolution in Romania. Massacre of democracy supporters in Tiananmen Square, Beijing, China

In 1971, Colonel Idi Amin Dada takes power in Uganda. Initially he is popular, but then creates a repressive regime under which many thousands are executed.

Haile Selassie I becomes Emperor of Ethiopia in 1930 and rules until 1974. During his long reign he achieves a great deal, but becomes unpopular when he begins to ignore problems at home while concentrating on foreign affairs.

In 1964 and 1977, Somalia and Ethiopia come into conflict over the Ogaden region of Ethiopia, which is inhabited largely by ethnic Somalis. These Ethiopian conscripts are on parade in Addis Ababa.

© DIAGRAM

Chronology

This is the insignia of the Eritrean Popular (or People's) LIberation Front (EPLF). The EPLF launches a rebel movement fighting for Eritrean independence from Ethiopia in the 1960s. In 1991, they achieve their goal when Eritrea is liberated from Ethiopia.

During Somalia's long civil war, arms pour in from both the former USSR and US, creating a culture of violence in which even children are involved.

In 1996, Burundi's Hutu president, Sylvestre Ntibantunganyu, accompanied by Tutsi soldiers, attends the funeral of 320 victims massacred by suspected Hutu rebels at a refugee camp in Burundi. Soon after this Ntibantunganyu is deposed by a coup led by former president Pierre Buyoya.

EAST AFRICAN EVENTS	WORLD EVENTS
1988 Fighting breaks out between Somali government and seccessionist SNM forces in former British Somaliland	**1990** Gulf War begins after Iraq invades Kuwait. IRA bomb Stock Exchange, London
1990 Prodemocracy and antigovernment riots in Kenya	
1991–1996	
1991 Afar guerillas in Djibouti demand multiparty politics. Mengistu loses control of Ethiopia; end of civil war: Eritrean liberation. Multiparty politics allowed in Kenya. Civil war in Somalia after Barre is ousted by rebel *clan* groups; former British Somaliland declares independence as Somaliland Republic. Ugandan Asians invited to return	East and West Germany reunited. Breakup of USSR. All apartheid legislation repealed in South Africa. End of Gulf War. Breakup of Yugoslavia; war erupts in Croatia and Slovenia
1992 Tutsi are massacred in Rwanda. First multiparty elections held in Djibouti. Civil war in Somalia leads to famine; UN and US intervene. Multiparty politics introduced in Tanzania	Formal end to Cold War announced. Riots in LA. War in former Yugoslavia spreads to Bosnia
1993 Burundi Hutu president killed – probably assassinated. Ertirea officially independent. Ugandan monarchies restored; nonparty elections held. Fighting between UN troops and Somali rebels led by Gen. Farrah Aideed. Multiparty elections in Seychelles	Israeli-PLO peace agreement. World Trade Center bomb kills six in US. 400 US Federal agents beseige religious cult in Waco, Texas
1994 Afar rebels end insurrection in Djibouti. Rwandan and Burundi Hutu presidents assassinated; in Rwanda, the Hutu army attacks Tutsi and moderate Hutu; over 500,000 people are massacred in three months. Short-lived cease-fire in Somalia; UN begins to withdraw. Ethiopian war crimes trial begins work	Nelson Mandela and ANC win first nonracial elections in South Africa. US intervention in Haiti. Cease-fire announced by IRA. Severe flooding in northern Italy
1995 Ethnic violence between Hutu and Tutsi spreads to Burundi. Ugandan and Sudanese troops	Peace agreement in former Yugoslavia. France

EAST AFRICAN EVENTS	WORLD EVENTS
clash in Sudan. Massacre at Hutu refugee camp in Rwanda. Aideed declares himself "president" of Somalia, but effective power remains with the clan leaders	carries out nuclear tests in Pacific. Israeli prime minister assassinated
1996 Rwandan war crimes tribunal set up. Violence escalates in Burundi; Rwandan Hutu refugees forcibly repatriated; military coup in Burundi, neighboring countries impose economic sanctions. Aideed dies in fighting; his son, Hussein Muhammad Aideed succeeds him as president. Over 600 drown in Tanzanian ferry disaster on Lake Victoria	IRA end cease-fire. TWA airliner explodes off Long Island, NY, killing 230 passengers and crew. Outbreaks of Arab-Israeli violence increase in Israel and Palestine

Julius Nyerere, a leading campaigner for independence from colonial rule, is the president of Tanzania from 1964 until 1985. He introduces policies of socialism and self-reliance to Tanzania between the 1960s and the 1980s.

COLONIAL OCCUPATION AND INDEPENDENCE

Country	Independence	Occupied*	Colonial powers
Burundi *(as part of Ruanda-Urundi)*	July 1, 1962	1890	Germany 1890–1919; Belgium 1919–1962
Djibouti *(as French Somaliland then French Territory of the Afars and the Issas)*	June 27, 1977	1884	France
Eritrea	May 24, 1993	1889	Italy 1889–1941; Britain 1941–1952; ruled by Ethiopia 1952–1993
Kenya	Dec 12, 1963	1895	Britain
Malawi *(as Nyasaland)*	July 6, 1964	1891	Britain
Rwanda *(as part of Ruanda-Urundi)*	July 1, 1962	1890	Germany 1890–1919; Belgium 1919–1962
Seychelles	June 29, 1976	1742	France 1742–1814; Britain 1814–1976
Somalia *(As British Somaliland)*	June 26, 1960	1884	Britain
Somalia *(As Italian Somaliland)*	July 1, 1960	1886	Italy 1886–1941; 1950–1960; Britain 1941–1950
Tanzania *(as Tanganyika)*	Dec 9, 1961	1885	Germany 1885–1920; Britain 1920–1961
Tanzania *(Zanzibar)*	Dec 10, 1963	1890	Britain
Uganda *(as Uganda Protectorate)*	Oct 9, 1962	1888	Britain

* The years given for the beginning of colonial occupation of the modern-day nations are those by which a significant area of coastal and hinterland territory had been effectively occupied by a colonial power.

© DIAGRAM

Pictorial history

A nineteenth-century Nyamwezi carving *(left)* given as a gift to encourage trade. The Nyamwezi people were pioneers of East and Central African trade.

Above is a prayer book written in Geez – an ancient Ethiopian language rarely spoken today.

Many kingdoms flourished between lakes Victoria and Albert. One of the most important of these was the Kingdom of Bunyoro, which was established in the sixteenth century. The Bunyoro king *(right)* is still an important figure in modern Ugandan society, though his role is largely ceremonial.

This historic painting captures the Ethiopian defeat of Italian forces at the Battle of Adowa (modern Adwa) in 1896.

Another kingdom that flourished between lakes Victoria and Albert is the Bugandan Kingdom, which was established over five hundred years ago and still exists today as part of Uganda. The Bugandans were visited by the explorers Speke and Grant, shown here at the king's palace *(left)*.

Since the colonial era, cash cropping has increased dramatically in East Africa. The most common cash crops are tea, shown being picked on the left, and coffee.

This child *(above)* has been orphaned by the recent conflicts between the Hutu and Tutsi in Rwanda and Burundi.

East Africa was one of the first homes of early humankind. This artist's impression *(right)* is of *Australopithecus afarensis*, a 3-million-year-old skeleton that was found in Ethiopia.

Lake Albert
Masindi
Lake Kyoga
Mt Elgon ▲
Jinja
Kampala
Lake Edward
Kisumu
Lake Victoria
Kigali
Lake Kivu
Olduvai Gorge ■
Mwanza
Lake Eyasi
Bujumbura
Ujiji
Tabora
Lake Tanganyika
Lake Rukwa
Lake Nyasa (Malawi)
Lilongwe

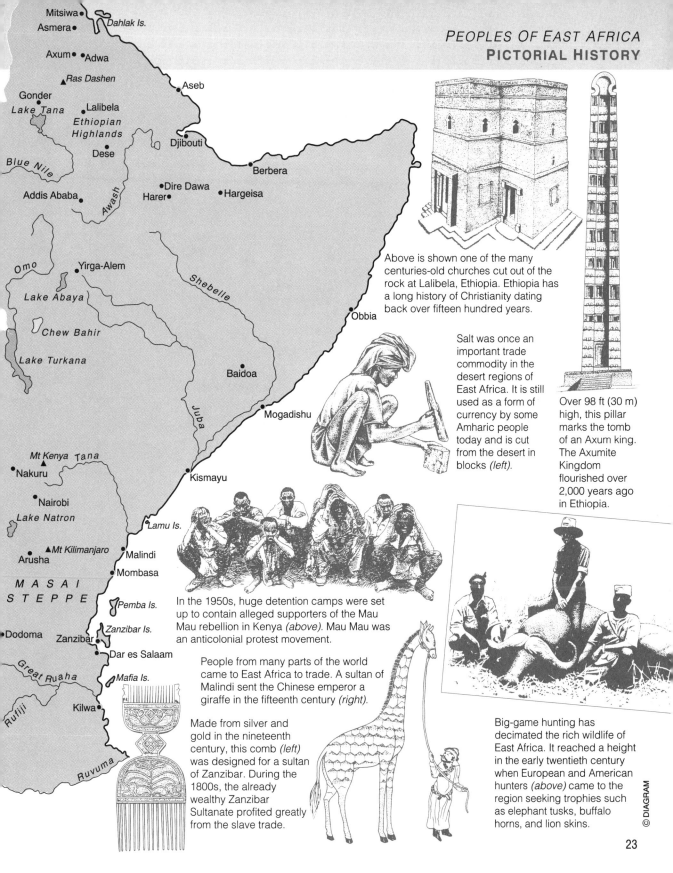

Map labels:

Mitsiwa
Asmera
Dahlak Is.
Axum • Adwa
Ras Dashen
Aseb
Gonder
Lake Tana
Lalibela
Ethiopian Highlands
Dese
Djibouti
Blue Nile
Berbera
Addis Ababa
Awash
Dire Dawa
Harer • Hargeisa
Omo
Yirga-Alem
Shebelle
Lake Abaya
Chew Bahir
Obbia
Lake Turkana
Baidoa
Juba
Mogadishu
Mt Kenya Tana
Nakuru
Kismayu
Nairobi
Lake Natron
Lamu Is.
Mt Kilimanjaro
Malindi
Arusha
Mombasa
MASAI STEPPE
Pemba Is.
Zanzibar Is.
Dodoma
Zanzibar
Dar es Salaam
Great Ruaha
Mafia Is.
Kilwa
Rufiji
Ruvuma

Above is shown one of the many centuries-old churches cut out of the rock at Lalibela, Ethiopia. Ethiopia has a long history of Christianity dating back over fifteen hundred years.

Salt was once an important trade commodity in the desert regions of East Africa. It is still used as a form of currency by some Amharic people today and is cut from the desert in blocks (left).

Over 98 ft (30 m) high, this pillar marks the tomb of an Axum king. The Axumite Kingdom flourished over 2,000 years ago in Ethiopia.

In the 1950s, huge detention camps were set up to contain alleged supporters of the Mau Mau rebellion in Kenya (above). Mau Mau was an anticolonial protest movement.

People from many parts of the world came to East Africa to trade. A sultan of Malindi sent the Chinese emperor a giraffe in the fifteenth century (right).

Made from silver and gold in the nineteenth century, this comb (left) was designed for a sultan of Zanzibar. During the 1800s, the already wealthy Zanzibar Sultanate profited greatly from the slave trade.

Big-game hunting has decimated the rich wildlife of East Africa. It reached a height in the early twentieth century when European and American hunters (above) came to the region seeking trophies such as elephant tusks, buffalo horns, and lion skins.

© DIAGRAM

23

Distribution of peoples

1 Falasha

The Falasha (or Beta Israel) live in the highlands of northern Ethiopia, although many have recently emigrated to Israel. Most Falasha speak either Tigrinya or Amharic – depending on where they live in Ethiopia – or, more recently, Hebrew. The Falasha are a Jewish people but have only been in contact with world Judaism for the last hundred years.

3 Afar

The Afar (or Danakil) live in the desert regions of Ethiopia, Eritrea, and Djibouti. The majority of the Afar are *nomadic pastoralists*. Historically, the Afar formed various sultanates but are now almost semiautonomous. The Afar are Muslims and speak a language also called Afar.

4 Oromo

The Oromo (or Galla) live in southeastern Ethiopia and northern Kenya. In the past, they formed many Muslim kingdoms. The Oromo language is also called Oromo. Most Oromo follow either Islam or Christianity, and a minority still practice the Oromo religion.

5 Somalis

The majority of Somalis live in Somalia. Others form considerable minorities in Ethiopia and northern Kenya and a few also live in Djibouti. The Somalis have a distinctive social structure organized around *clans*. They speak a language also called Somali. The vast majority of Somalis are Muslims.

2 Amhara

The Amhara live mostly in the highlands of northern Ethiopia. Although the Amhara only form around one-third of Ethiopia's population, they dominate the country's political and economic life, both now and historically under the Ethiopian Empire. Amharic is the language of the Amhara. The majority of the Amhara are Christians and Christianity has played a major role in Amhara culture for many centuries.

ሱ፡ወአጠየተ፡ታሎ፡ጥቤ
ሎ፡ሶበ፡ታተርብ
ጸበ፡ምሥጥራ፡ወ
ከ፡በሀ፡ከመ፡ህ
ከ፡ዘየኒይስከተ
ተርበናተከ፡
አሰ፡እተከ፡
ንሕ፡እሬኤ፡
ጠዉ፡ሠግ
ከርስቶስ
በወሐ፡ሰ
ልዉ፡በ
ልኦ፡ሕገ
አሰ፡በጸ
ወእመ
መ፡በየስ
ጽሕ፡ነተ

6 Karamojong

The Karamojong live in northeastern Uganda. They are a *seminomadic, pastoral* people to whom cattle are very important. The different Karamojong groups speak various dialects of the Karamajong language. Few Karamojong have converted to Christianity or Islam; their own religion is most frequently followed.

Gulf of Aden

5

5

SOMALIA

5

5

Shebelle

5

14 Swahili
The Swahili live along the coast of Kenya and Tanzania and on offshore islands such as Pemba and Zanzibar. Swahilis are of mixed Black African, Arab, and Persian descent. The Swahili have a long history of international trading, and, as a result of this, the Swahili language is widely used throughout East Africa as a common or trading language. The vast majority of Swahili people are Muslim.

13 Nyamwezi
The Nyamwezi live in west-central Tanzania. They speak dialects of the Nyamwezi language. In the past, the Nyamwezi were pioneers of long-distance trade in East and Central Africa. Although a few Nyamwezi are Muslim or Christian, the majority follow the Nyamwezi religion.

9 Kikuyu
The Kikuyu (or Gikuyu) are the largest ethnic group in Kenya. The Kikuyu were often at the forefront of resistance to British rule during the colonial era. The Kikuyu language is also called Kikuyu. Many Kikuyu are Christians and have established their own, independent, churches. A few follow the Kikuyu religion.

12 Hutu and Tutsi
The Hutu and Tutsi make up the bulk of the populations of Rwanda and Burundi. Their culture and history are closely related and interwoven. Historically, the Tutsi dominated the Hutu but more recently there have been many, often violent, reversals of the balance of power. Both peoples speak the same language, called Rundi in Burundi and Rwanda in Rwanda. The majority of Hutu and Tutsi are Christians, but the indigenous religion still has many followers.

8 Ganda
The Ganda (or Baganda) live mostly in the northwestern lakes region of Uganda. They established a highly centralized monarchy under the Buganda Kingdom, which is now part of modern Uganda. The Ganda language is also called Ganda. Relatively recently, many Ganda have become Christian or Muslim, but the Ganda religion is itself still widely practiced.

11 Maasai
The Maasai live in a region that spans the border of Kenya and Tanzania. They are largely *nomadic pastoralists* who herd cattle but are increasingly becoming settled and sometimes practice agriculture. The Maasai speak a language called Maa. The Maasai have mostly resisted conversion to Islam or Christianity and largely follow their own religion.

7 Nyoro
The Nyoro (or Banyoro) are from the northwestern lakes region of Uganda. They once formed the Bunyoro-Kitara Empire and later the Bunyoro Kingdom, now part of Uganda. The Nyoro speak a language that is also called Nyoro. Most Nyoro are either Christian or Muslim, but the Nyoro religion is still followed.

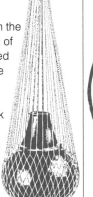

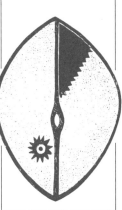

10 East African Asians
Many Asians, largely from India, have settled in East Africa during and since the colonial era. They form a small, but influential, minority in Kenya, Tanzania, and Uganda. East African Asians speak a variety of Indian languages, in particular Gujarati or Punjabi. Many also speak an African language such as Swahili and, or, English. Most East African Asians are either Hindu or Muslim though a minority follow the *Zoroastrian* religion.

© DIAGRAM

Introduction

The peoples of East Africa reflect a wide variety of lifestyles and cultures. This book describes a selected sample of these cultures, where possible detailing contemporary changes and the effects they have had on people's lives.

The peopling of East Africa

East Africa was one of the first homes of the human race. Over two million years ago, remotely ancestral types of humans appeared to have inhabited East Africa. More direct ancestors of *Homo sapiens* (early humans) evolved into *Homo sapiens sapiens* (modern humans) some 50,000 years ago in East Africa. It is not clear, however, how the people who presently inhabit East Africa relate to these early ancestors.

The original (human) inhabitants of East Africa were probably ancestors of the Khoisan people – *hunter-gatherers* distinctive for their short stature and use of languages that contain click sounds. The Sandawe and maybe the Hadza of Tanzania are probably the only direct descendants remaining in East Africa today. Over many hundreds of years, these people retreated or were absorbed as others migrated into the area. This peopling of East Africa was carried out by three main African groups: the Cushitic peoples; the Nilotic peoples; and the Bantu peoples. These groupings are based on cultural and linguistic similarities and comprise the ancestors of most present-day East Africans – the Black Africans.

The Cushites originated from the Ethiopian Highlands and were the first food producers in East Africa. They spread out from their original dispersal site to occupy most of northeastern Africa and some also migrated farther south. The Cushites had already reached the Kenyan Highlands by c. 1000 BCE. The Oromo of Ethiopia and northeast Kenya are Eastern Cushites. The Nilotes originated from the southwestern borders of the Ethiopian Highlands – the Nile River region of southern Sudan. The Nilotes are further divided into three branches based on where they migrated to: the Highland and Plains Nilotes (who are also part Cushitic) and the River-Lake Nilotes. Between 1000 BCE and 1500 CE, the Highland and Plains Nilotes migrated into the highlands and plains of Kenya and Tanzania. The Maasai and the Karamojong are Plains Nilotes. The River-Lake Nilotes, however, followed the Nile Valley and settled in the lakes region of northern Uganda or traveled north to present-day southern Sudan. The Bantu people originated in eastern Nigeria. At first, they spread through the equatorial *rainforest* belt and then, between 500 BCE and 300 CE, eastward and southward into East and Southern Africa. Later migrations – from the south to the east – further dispersed them throughout the region. The Kikuyu, Ganda, Nyoro, and Nyamwezi people are all Bantu in origin, as are the majority of East Africans.

Historical overview

The earliest civilization in East Africa was the Axumite Kingdom, which emerged in Ethiopia in the 100s. This early state was the precursor of one of the longest lasting empires in the world: the Ethiopian Empire, which lasted until the deposing of Emperor Haile Selassie I in 1974. Farther south, many Bantu kingdoms such as Bunyoro, Buganda, Toro, and Ruanda-Urundi arose in the second millennium. Meanwhile, the coast attracted Arab, Persian, and Indian traders and settlers and became an international trading center with many substantial ports. Gold and ivory were the staple African exports and textiles, metalware, and luxury goods such as pottery and porcelain were the main imports.

During the eighteenth century, slave trading in East Africa began to grow. The Europeans needed slaves for their new colonies in the Americas and the Arabs needed labor for their plantations on the coast and its islands. Although slavery was not new to Africa and some kingdoms flourished because of it, the slave trade caused great human suffering, distorted local economies, and increased conflict in the region. At its height in the 1860s, 70,000 slaves were being sold annually at the main market, on Zanzibar. The slave trade came to an end with the close of the nineteenth century.

Despite great resistance by its inhabitants, by 1914 all of East Africa except Ethiopia was under European colonial rule. Ethiopia was never colonized but was invaded and occupied by Italy between 1935 and 1941. European colonization greatly affected East Africa, setting the modern political boundaries and molding the region's economies into their present dependence on the export of raw materials rather than processed goods. By the 1970s, East Africa was independent again but as ten nations that had little to do with ethnic groupings or historical African states.

Geography

East Africa does not form a natural geographical region. Basically, however, it comprises the Horn of Africa (Somalia and neighboring regions of Ethiopia and Djibouti) and its immediate vicinity; the coast of Africa that is adjacent to the Indian Ocean as far south as Mozambique; the inland regions covered by the Great Rift Valley; and all the lands between these features. The Great Rift Valley is a depression that extends from the Jordan River Valley in southwest Asia across most of East Africa. In the past, it acted as a corridor facilitating the peopling of East Africa. The land of East Africa can be divided into four main categories: desert and semidesert; tropical *savanna* (grasslands with scattered trees and shrubs); forest; and mountainous regions. Important geographical features include the Ethiopian Highlands; the major rivers (Tana, Omo, Great Ruaha, Juba, and Shebelle, for example); the great lakes that are the sources of the Nile River (lakes Albert and Victoria, for example); the many offshore islands that dot the coast, such as Zanzibar, Mafia, and Pemba; and, of course, the Great Rift Valley.

Much of the Horn of Africa is semidesert, the vegetation is sparse, and there are periodic *droughts* (water shortages caused by periods of inadequate rainfall). There are few areas of real desert in East Africa and these are concentrated around the Horn, the Red Sea coast, and northern Kenya. The savanna lands are characterized by open woodlands and parklike grasslands. They include most of the highlands that occur in East Africa. Some of the world's highest mountains are in East Africa: for example, Mount Kilimanjaro, Mount Kenya, and Mount Elgon. Mountainous regions have their own distinct, high-altitude environments. Tropical forests cover some of the mountain slopes and valleys but there are relatively few large stretches of forest compared to other parts of Africa. A few small, pockets of dense rainforest remain on the western slopes of the Great Rift Valley – remnants of the rainforests that once stretched from Central Africa right across to the shores of Lake Victoria. Both the savanna and the forest lands have rainy and dry season cycles. Additionally, the *monsoon* (seasonal) winds of the Indian Ocean have been important historically as they aided the growth of trade with people from Asia.

People today

The population figures provided for each ethnic group are estimates from between 1980 and 1996. The peoples selected for inclusion tend to be distributed across more than one country. It is difficult, therefore, to use national censuses (which vary in frequency and amount from nation to nation) to gather up-to-date information about a people's numbers. Statistics have been taken instead from a variety of sociological and anthropological sources; they have been included only to indicate the size and relative importance of a group.

The vast majority of East Africans are Black Africans. A considerable minority, however, are not. Arabs and Persians, who began to settle on the coast as early as the ninth century, intermarried with local people and gave rise to groups such as the Swahili. In the last hundred years, many Asians, mainly from India, and also Europeans have settled in East Africa and now form influential minorities in their adoptive countries. Through migration, conquest, and intermingling, the people of East Africa have diversified over the years into many different ethnic groups. It is difficult and often inappropriate, therefore, to classify people according to physical appearance or race. Also, national boundaries were colonial inventions and do not necessarily relate to ethnic groups or historical African states. Ethnic groups are more a matter of cultural, linguistic, historical, religious, and perceived similarities than race or nationality. Nevertheless, ethnicity remains a potent force in East Africa today, the recent troubles in Rwanda and Burundi between the Hutu and the Tutsi bear witness to this.

Hundreds of languages are spoken in East Africa. Many are particular to certain ethnic groups, while others have many speakers due to historical factors. Swahili is spoken widely, as it was an important trading language and is now used as a common language. Also, Muslims often learn Arabic, the language of the Islamic holy book, the *Koran*. English has been used in East Africa since the colonial era. Many East African Asians speak one or more Indian languages. The result of this diversity is that many East Africans are multilingual – they speak more than one language.

There are also many religions in East Africa. The bulk of these are particular to certain ethnic groups. The two most widely practiced religions in East Africa, however, are Islam and Christianity, sometimes practiced in conjuction with an African religion. At least 1,000 years ago, Islam was introduced by Arabic traders who came to settle on the coast. It did not spread much beyond these initial areas until the nineteenth century though. Ethiopia has a long history of Christianity extending back nearly two thousand years. Other parts of East Africa were introduced to Christianity by European missionaries in the nineteenth century.

Lifestyles

The population of East Africa is roughly eighty-five-percent rural. This statistic hides a huge variety of lifestyles. Many people are farmers; others are traders, scholars, weavers, doctors, artists, writers, teachers, miners – there are as many occupations as you would expect to find in any contemporary society. It is difficult, therefore, to describe the typical lifestyle of any specific group of people. Nevertheless, some attempt has been made to describe common lifestyles and occupations.

To some extent, geography determines the lifestyles of agricultural peoples. Most East African soils are capable of *subsistence agriculture* at least. Until recently, the most common system of agriculture was *shifting cultivation.* A patch of land is cleared, cultivated, and then abandoned when exhausted. In the forest regions, this is combined with a technique called *slash and burn* to clear the land of its cover. Although labor intensive, such methods are ideally suited to the tropics. They allow the soil to recuperate, they conserve the environment, and the burning of vegetation fixes nutrients in the soil. In regions where vegetation is sparse and rainfall irregular, people have developed systems of *pastoral nomadism* – livestock herding in which herders travel with their animals in search of pasture and water.

Recent changes

Agriculture has undergone many changes in East Africa. Larger farms, plantations, cash crops, and *monoculture* (one-crop) farming systems are all relatively recent changes. They have had both positive and negative effects. Cash crops for export such as coffee, tea, tobacco, and sugar bring welcome foreign currency into many East African countries. Dependency on exports of raw materials rather than processed goods, however, leaves economies at the mercy of changes in the world market. This is why East African countries have tried to develop other sources of income and establish manufacturing and processing industries. Furthermore, soil erosion was not a problem historically as indigenous farming methods protected the fragile topsoil. Intensive farming techniques have changed this. Soils not given time to recuperate become increasingly poorer and the loss of natural vegetative cover has left them vulnerable to erosion. *Deforestation* in the forested mountain regions has had a similar effect.

A growing urban population has been a part of all these changes. *Urbanization* is not foreign to East Africa. The Swahili people, for example, have lived in towns for hundreds of years, and many busy modern cities are based on ancient trading centers. The pace of urbanization, however, has increased markedly as people migrate from rural areas in search of better prospects in the cities. This has put more pressure on rural areas to feed the growing cities, while lack of employment in urban areas has meant the development of an urban poor. Conversely, *underemployment* (although few people are totally unemployed, many do not have enough work to provide for their needs) has led to thriving urban informal sectors in which people create their own job opportunities – by illicit trading, for example. These so-called "black markets" are an important source of income to many urban East Africans.

Tourism has grown markedly in East Africa since the colonial era. The rich wildlife of Kenya and Tanzania, in particular, has been decimated by big-game hunters of the colonial era and, more recently, by poaching and smuggling. National parks and game reserves now protect many species, but have often led to the eviction or banning of local people who have managed to coexist with the wildlife for hundreds of years. The growth of tourism, while bringing foreign currency into the region, has highlighted the presence of conflicting interests. Visitors are often eager to see what they view as the "traditional Africa" while African governments are often at pains to present a more contemporary image of their country. Furthermore, the huge numbers of people attracted by the region's flora and fauna actually threaten its existence. In response to this, some countries have begun providing more expensive, upmarket facilities to cater for fewer – but higher spending – tourists.

© DIAGRAM

Afar

Afar timeline

by 1000s Afar settled in present lands
1200s– Afar Muslim states at war with
  1600s Christian Ethiopia
1884 French Somaliland
  (Djibouti) formed
1935– Ethiopia invaded and
  1941 occupied by Italy
1961 Eritreans begin struggle for
  independence from Ethiopia
1967 French Somaliland renamed
  French Territory of the Afars
  and the Issas
1974 Military coup in Ethiopia
  overthrows Haile Selassie I
1975 Afar Liberation Front (ALF)
  formed. ALF active on
  Ethiopian-Djibouti border
1977 Djibouti wins independence.
  Maj. Mengistu Haile Mariam
  takes power in Ethiopia
1979 In Djibouti, Afar form illegal
  prodemocracy movement
1980s Severe *droughts* cause
  famine in Ethiopia
1981 Djibouti made a one-party state
1987 In Ethiopia, autonomous Afar
  region created
1991 Mengistu loses power; end of
  civil war; Eritrean liberation In
  Djibouti, 100 Afar dissidents
  arrested; Afar commence
  rebel activities
1992 Unsound multiparty elections
  end one-party state in Djibouti
1993 Eritrea officially
  independent from Ethiopia
1994 Afar state created in Ethiopia.
  Peace talks end Afar
  insurrection in Djibouti
1995 300 former Afar rebels join
  Djibouti army

T he Afar (or Danakil) live in the Danakil Desert in Eritrea and Ethiopia, and in neighboring Djibouti. There are approximately 700,000 Afar.

History

The ancestors of the Afar were settled livestock raisers in Ethiopia, but before 1000 they gradually shifted to a *nomadic* (unsettled) lifestyle and moved from the highlands to the area they occupy today. Their history has often been a violent one marked by fighting with invading armies and, later, imperial and national governments. Disputes with neighboring peoples have also continued until well into the twentieth century.

RECENT EVENTS In 1975, an Afar nationalist insurrection movement began in Ethiopia. The Afar Liberation Front (ALF) was established after an unsuccessful rebellion led by a former Afar sultan. Although the military government established the Autonomous Region of Assab (modern Aseb), the Afar were not satisfied with the degree of autonomy they were given and the insurrection continued until Eritrea became independent from Ethiopia in the early 1990s.

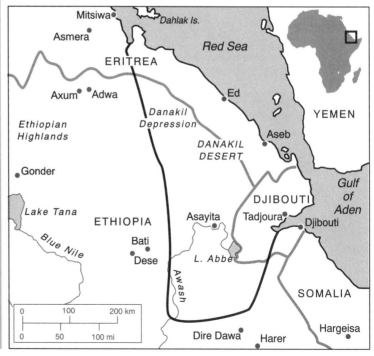

Camels with burdens
The camel is the essential beast of burden for *nomadic* peoples of the desert, like the Afar. The search for water dominates the lives of these people, and as they move the camels carry everything, including, as shown here, the light poles and mats that are used to build the Afar houses.

The Afar make up about half the population (along with the Somalis) of the country of Djibouti, which gained its independence from France in 1977. There have been clashes between the Afar and the Somalis, and a three-year uprising by the Afar, which ended in 1994.

Language
The Afar language (or Danakil) is a Cushitic language.

Ways of life
NOMADIC PASTORALISM Although today some Afar have migrated to cities like Addis Ababa and the port of Djibouti, the majority have long been *nomadic pastoralists*, tending herds of goats, sheep, and cattle in the harsh desert. They move from one waterhole to the next, eking a subsistence living from the barren soil. As the dry season advances, most Afar head for the banks of the River Awash, where they make camps. Because this is the only important river in the region, they compete for the best places and carefully guard the positions they take along the banks. The Awash River rises in the mountains and carries a great deal of water, but the heat is so great that it never meets the sea, ending instead in Lake Abbe.

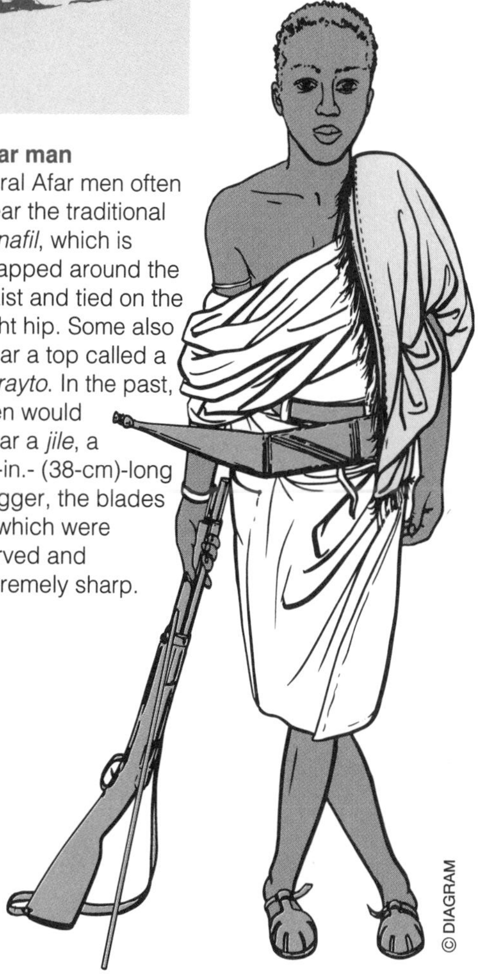

Afar man
Rural Afar men often wear the traditional *sanafil*, which is wrapped around the waist and tied on the right hip. Some also wear a top called a *harayto*. In the past, men would wear a *jile*, a 15-in.- (38-cm)-long dagger, the blades of which were curved and extremely sharp.

© DIAGRAM

33

Kwosso game
Kwosso is a fast ball game played by the Afar. The ball is made of rolled goatskins, and the object is to keep it away from the opposing teams. In the past, teams were made up of as many as one hundred players.

Afar woman
A married Afar woman customarily wears a black cloth, known as a *shash* or *mushal*, as a headdress.

The end of the dry season is hard on both the people and the animals. Food and grazing are scarce. Some Afar head for Asayita, regarded as the capital of the Afar, hoping to find land they can cultivate.

When the short rainy season arrives in November, most of the Afar move to higher ground. Mosquitoes and floods are the hazards of the plains in winter.

Like other nomadic peoples, the Afar carry their houses and beds with them. The Afar house is called an *ari* and is made with a number of flexible sticks, covered with mats. If the camp – known as the *burra*, and usually consisting of one or two ari – is to be occupied for some time, the Afar assemble beds for use inside the ari. These too are made with mats resting on pliable wooden sticks, and are cool and comfortable for sleeping.

The women are responsible for looking after the camp. They build the houses and beds, but they are also responsible for keeping the camp clean, taking care of the children, and looking after the animals.

The milk and hides of the livestock are used for the Afar's own needs and are also traded for grain and vegetables. Salt is also sold; blocks of it are dug out of the desert. The two main markets for selling and trading are Senbete and Bati, both in inland Ethiopia.

Social structure

SOCIAL STRUCTURE The Afar are organized into *clans*, groups of extended families who trace their descent from a common ancestor or ancestors. They also divide themselves between two classes: the *asaimara* (the "reds") and the *adoimara* (the "whites") or the lower class. The asaimara tend to be politically dominant; the adoimara are generally the workers.

Descent is traced through the male line, and it is said that men inherit strength of character from their fathers. Physical characteristics such as height, and also spiritual aspects are said to come from the mother.

The Afar practice *circumcision* rites on both boys and, much more controversially, the more serious operation on girls. A man is frequently judged for the bravery with which he bore the pain of circumcision. On becoming an adult, such a man would be able to marry the young woman of his choice, as he would be admired by his people. People ideally marry a partner from their own ethnic group, preferably a cousin. The emphasis on families leads to powerful feelings of loyalty.

POLITICAL STRUCTURE In the past, Afar society was organized into various sultanates, each of which comprised several villages. Each sultanate was headed by an appointed figure known as a *dardar*. Today, the Afar live in a semiautonomous region of federal Ethiopia.

Culture and religion

RELIGION The Afar were converted to Islam by Arabs in the tenth century. Although Islam is now of great importance to the Afar and they observe Muslim rules in most aspects of life, they have modified Islamic practices according to their own culture and religion, which is based on a Sky-god.

CLOTHING The basis of traditional Afar dress is the *sanafil*, a cloth tied around the waist: for men it is undyed, but women's sanafils are dyed brown using a dye produced from the bark of mimosa trees. Today, many women replace this brown cloth with brightly-colored, imported fabrics. "Western" dress is preferred by many Afar, especially those who live and work in the cities.

Scouring for salt
Some Afar search for salt, the only thing produced by the desert. Above, an Afar man chips away at a large block of salt.

Afar hairdo
This distinctive hairstyle is worn by many men following initiation, usually at around age fifteen. It is seen as a demonstration of manhood.

Ari
Light and portable, the *ari*, or Afar house, provides cool shelter from the blistering sun. The house can be built and dismantled quickly, a job usually reserved for women.

© DIAGRAM

35

East Africa: the birthplace of humanity

Over one hundred years ago, the naturalist Charles Darwin suggested that humans originated in Africa. We now know that this is probably true; scientific discoveries since the 1950s have shown, in fact, that the earliest human beings and their immediate ancestors most likely evolved in East Africa. The oldest known fossils of human ancestors have been discovered in Ethiopia, Kenya, and Tanzania. These precursors of present-day human beings are collectively called "hominids," from the Latin word "homo," meaning "man." Scientists group humans, apes, monkeys, and several other animals, such as lemurs, together as primates. They believe the primates all had a common ancestor, which lived in East Africa more than five million years ago.

4.4 million years ago, 500,000 years before the previously known earliest hominid. Several species of australopithecines have been found, some in East Africa and some in southern Africa. Before ramidus the oldest known hominid was Australopithecus afarensis ("southern ape of Afar"). In 1974, a partial afarensis skeleton, three-million-years old, was found in northern Ethiopia (in the Afar region) and was nicknamed "Lucy." Both ramidus and afarensis were lightly built and only about 4 ft (1.3 m) tall. So was the next oldest species, Australopithecus africanus, which probably lived from three million to one million years ago. A later species, boisei, was discovered in East Africa in 1959; it was named after a British industrialist, Charles Boise, who funded East African fossil hunts.

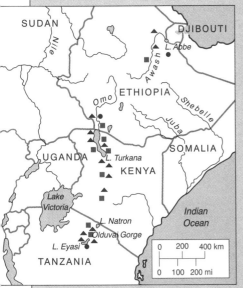

Major sites
This map shows some of the major sites of early-human fossil finds in East Africa.

Key
- ▲ Australopith-ecine sites
- ■ Homo erectus and Homo habilis sites
- ● Homo sapiens sites

The earliest hominids

Fossilized bones of several specimens of the earliest known hominid were discovered in eastern Ethiopia by American anthropologists in 1992–94. This creature has been named Australopithecus ramidus (ramidus means "root" in the language of the Afar who live in the area; Australopithecus means "southern ape"). This species lived about

Australopithecus afarensis
This artist's reconstruction compares afarensis with, in the background, a modern male human.

The first humans

After the australopithecines, all our supposed ancestors are grouped in the scientific genus Homo. *The first known species of* Homo *was* habilis, *or "handyman."* Habilis *remains were discovered in Tanzania in 1961, and it probably lived about two million years ago. It is thought that the earliest known toolkit, containing pebbles chipped into tool-like shapes, was made by* habilis; *these and other artifacts from what is known as the Oldowan Culture have been found in the Olduvai Gorge in Tanzania.* Habilis *is also believed to have built shelters to live in and hunted for food. Evidence of early campsites suggests that the earliest human settlements might have been at Olduvai Gorge. The remains of very early fences and even a stone circle that was probably the foundation for a hut have been found, making it, at nearly two-million-years old, the oldest known human-built structure.*

The next hominid was Homo erectus, *"upright man." Its earliest fossil was found near the western shore of Lake Turkana in Kenya, and is 1.6-million-years old.* Homo erectus *spread from East Africa over Europe and Asia, and persisted until about 200,000 years ago. Modern humans belong*

Pebble tool
This pebble tool is one of the many artifacts found at Olduvai Gorge. It was probably made by *Homo habilis* 2.5 million years go.

to the species Homo sapiens sapiens, *which appeared sometime between 400,000 and 300,000 years ago in Africa, Europe, and Asia, and are almost certainly descended from* erectus.

Fossil hunters

Much of the research into early humans in East Africa was carried out by Anglo-Kenyan anthropologists of the Leakey family – Louis and Mary Leakey and their sons Richard and Jonathan – and their Kenyan co-workers, including Bernard Ngeneo and Kimoya Kimeu, who made some of the most important finds. One of Kimeu's most important discoveries was a Homo erectus *skeleton, 1.5-million-years old, found in 1984 near Lake Turkana in northern Kenya.*

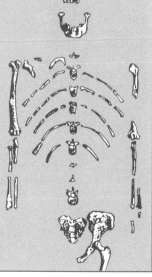

Olduvai Gorge (left)
Olduvai Gorge, in northern Tanzania, is a deep cleft in the ground in the Great Rift Valley. Its cliffs are 330 ft (130 m) high and expose deposits ranging in age from 10,000 to 2,000,000 years old. Stone tools made by members of the Oldowan Culture 2.5 million years ago, have been found in Olduvai Gorge.
Lucy (right)
This skeleton, nicknamed "Lucy," is of the genus *Australopithecus afarensis* and was found in 1974 in northern Ethiopia.

Amhara

T here are about fifteen million Amhara, who make up roughly thirty-five percent of Ethiopia's population and dominate the country's political and economic life. Most live in the rolling hills of the plateau to the north of Addis Ababa (Ethiopia's capital).

History

The Amhara are a Cushitic people whose ancestors lived in Ethiopia over two thousand years ago. The Cushites were the first food producers in Africa. The facts that for thousands of years the region has been the site of international trade routes, and that the Amhara have been influenced by the Semitic cultures of Arabia, suggest that Arabs and Greeks are probably among the Amhara's ancestors as well as Africans.

The earliest Ethiopian kingdom was centred on Axum (in what is now Tigre province). According to tradition, the Queen of Sheba (now part of Yemen) visited King Solomon in Jerusalem, and together they produced a son, Menelik. Solomon allowed Menelik to make a copy of the Ark of the Covenant, one of the most sacred Jewish objects. Menelik secretly exchanged the copy for the real Ark and took it to Axum, where he founded a kingdom, reigning between about 975 and 950 BCE.

Amhara timeline

100	Axumite Kingdom emerges
300s	Axumites issue gold currency
c. 320– 355	Rule of Ezana, first Christian king of the Axumite Kingdom
640 on	Rise of Islam; slow decline of Axumite Kingdom
1117	Zagwe dynasty founded in Ethiopia
1268	Zagwe dynasty overthrown
1270	Amhara Solomonic dynasty established
1400s– 1500s	Expansion of Ethiopian Empire through conquest
1700s	Ethiopia splits into several separate states
1855– 1930	Series of Ethiopian rulers rise to reclaim Empire in an attempt to prevent colonialism
1896	Battle of Adowa (modern Adwa): Italians defeated by Ethiopians
1930	Emperor Haile Selassie I begins reign
1935– 1941	Ethiopia invaded and occupied by Italy
1961	Eritrean rebels launch independence movement
1964	Ethiopia at war with Somalia
1970s	*Drought* and famine in Ethiopia
1974	Military coup overthrows Haile Selassie; socialist state declared
1977	Somalia invades Ethiopia. Maj. Mengistu Haile Mariam takes power in Ethiopia.
1980s	Drought and famine in Ethiopia
1991	Mengistu loses power; end of civil war for Eritrean liberation
1993	Eritrea offficially independent from Ethiopia
1994	Ethiopia organized into nine states based on ethnicity; widespread Amhara lose out

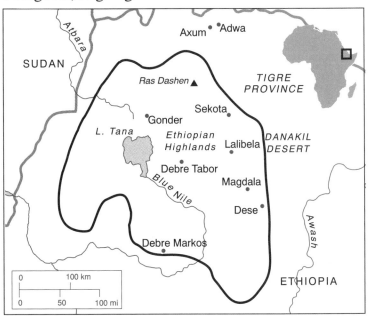

Historical records place the emergence of this kingdom in the 100s CE, however. The Axumite Kingdom grew to dominate much of what is now Ethiopia and southern Sudan and had great influence over southern Arabia. When the Axumite Kingdom's power declined from about 400, the Amhara from the south of the kingdom gradually gained political dominance over the Ethiopian Highlands. After Syrians converted Ezana, king of Axum 320–55, to Christianity, the Amhara gradually adopted the religion too. The spread of Islam in surrounding areas from the seventh century resulted in the isolation of the Amhara until the arrival of the Portuguese in the 1500s.

For centuries, emperors ruled Ethiopia, many of whom claimed to be descended from King Solomon and the Queen of Sheba, the dynasty having been restored in 1270 by King Yekuno Amlak. This Solomonic dynasty survived both Muslim encroachment and European colonization (apart from Italian occupation from 1935 to 1941) until 1974 when the Emperor Haile Selassie I was overthrown by the military in an initially popular revolt.

RECENT EVENTS The military government claimed to follow a Marxist ideology, seeking popular support by pursuing land reform. Military rule was often ruthless, however, with attacks not only on the landowning class but on all opposition, especially peoples seeking independence or autonomy from what they regarded as centuries of Amhara domination. In 1991, the military was overthrown and Eritrea – after a thirty-year civil war – was liberated from Ethiopia.

Language

Since about the fourteenth century, the Amhara's language has been Amharic, now Ethiopia's official language. Amharic is a Semitic language related to Geez, the ancient language of Ethiopia that is still used by the church today and which also forms the basis of the Amharic system of writing, but is rarely used in speech.

Processional cross
Elaborate crosses such as these are carried in processions held at Christmas and *Epiphany* (a Christian festival held on January 6 to commemorate the revelation of Jesus as Christ and his baptism). Such crosses are often protected from the Sun by an accompanying umbrella bearer.

© DIAGRAM

39

George and the dragon
Saint George (or Ghiorghis) is the patron saint of Ethiopia. This nineteenth-century picture is from the seventeenth-century church of Debre Berhan Selassie in the Gonder region of Ethiopia. Drawn on canvas fixed directly on to the wall, it shows Saint George slaying the dragon.

Amharic script
The Amharic script developed in Ethiopia over two thousand years ago and it is still used today. It is a modified version of an ancient Arabian script.

ሊ፡ወአጠየቀ፡ታሉ፡ወይቢ
ሉ፡ኦበ፡ታቀርብ፡ቀርበነክ፡
ደበ፡ምሥየራ፡ወተዘአር
ክ፡በሀየ፡ካመኮ፡ህየ፡እቷ
ክ፡ዘየጐይስክ፡ላጉግ፡ህየ፡
ቀርበናቴክ፡ወተዐረት፡ም
ስሊ፡እቷክ፡፡ወይእዚኌ፡አ
ጐስ፡እረኢ፡በዙጐን፡ይቶዉ
ጠዉ፡ሥጋሁ፡ለእገዚእነ፡
ክርስቶስ፡፡እሞ፡እንክ፡ተ
በወሕ፡ለሐየር፡እንዘ፡ይት
ሏዉ፡በዝነቴ፡ላግየ፡ዘአ

Ways of life

AGRICULTURE Nearly ninety percent of the Amhara are rural. The Ethiopian Highlands, where most Amhara live, is high, bleak, and hilly and many Amhara can grow just enough food for themselves and their families. Until the 1974 revolution, an unequal relationship was maintained between the (often absentee) landlords and sharecropping farmers, many of whom were in a virtual state of slavery as a result of accumulated debts. The revolution did not improve the circumstances of the farmers, only changed them: rural officials maintained strict control, farmers were forced into villages and large-scale, state-controlled farms, or sent to face the alien conditions of the remote south of Ethiopia where many died.

Amhara farmers grow barley, corn, millet, wheat, and, *teff* (a small grain rich in protein and iron) as well as beans, peppers, and other vegetables. Lowland farmers are able to produce two crops a year, but in the colder and less fertile highlands only a single crop is achieved. Oxen are used for plowing, though the poorer farmers may have to borrow or hire oxen for this purpose. Poultry, sheep, and goats are commonly kept, as are donkeys and mules – for transportation. Wild coffee, which originates in Ethiopia, is gathered, though it is generally of poor quality. The basic diet consists of vegetable or meat stews, accompanied by *injera* (a pancakelike fermented bread made from teff), coffee, beer, mead, or milk.

The revolution, civil war, and *droughts* (periods of inadequate rainfall) have all had their effect on farming in Ethiopia. Throughout the 1980s drought, rebel and government troop activities, inadequate infrastructure, and bureaucratic indifference all conspired to trigger a major famine during which many Amhara and other Ethiopians lost their lives or became refugees or migrants. Aid programmes since the 1980s have been aimed at small-scale farmers in the hope that they can be prosperous enough to be vulnerable to famine no longer.

DIVISION OF LABOR Men's primary responsibility is tilling the soil and caring for the larger animals. From the age of seven boys, are expected to work, at first helping to look after smaller animals and later herding cattle. Amhara girls over the age of seven are expected to help with the housework. Amhara women have many responsibilities, including cooking, making beer, collecting fuel (dried animal dung and wood), taking water from the nearest well or stream, spinning cotton, weaving mats and baskets, and caring for the children.

Social structure

A typical Amhara household consists of a husband (generally regarded as head of the family) and wife, their children, and other unmarried or elderly relatives.

Social and community life is centered on the local church. Marriages are generally arranged by the families, with boys usually marrying between seventeen and twenty-two, and girls sometimes as young as fourteen. Civil marriages are most typical, but some Amhara marry in church, though after such marriages divorce is prohibited. Two wedding feasts follow, one held by each family. A week after the birth of a baby a priest visits to bless and, if the child is a boy, to *circumcise* it. The mother and baby remain in seclusion for forty days after the birth, finally emerging to go to church for the baptism. When a person dies, a priest officiates at the funeral. A forty-day period of intense mourning follows, after which the priest holds a memorial service.

Culture and religion

RELIGION Christianity has been the religion of the Amhara for many centuries and the church is widely regarded as the guardian of Amhara culture. Most Amhara are members of the *Towahedo* (Orthodox) Christian Church which maintains close links with the Egyptian *Coptic* Church. There are numerous religious festivals – with Easter and *Epiphany* (the revelation and baptism of Christ) the most important – that are celebrated not only with religious services but with feasting and dancing.
ART Amhara art is closely linked with religion, and the Amhara decorate their churches with elaborate paintings, many of which were commissioned by wealthy landlords. Ethiopian church art is similar to that of other Orthodox churches and the influence of this style still persists.

Amharic homes
In general, Amhara houses are circular with walls made of *wattle-and-daub*, sometimes of stone, and with a thatched roof – the frame of which is supported by a central post.

Salt trading
Salt is one form of currency used by the Amhara. It is cut in blocks from the Danakil Desert in northeastern Ethiopia.

© DIAGRAM

The early Christian Church in Ethiopia

About half the people of two East African countries, Ethiopia and Eritrea, are Christians, and the story of their religion begins almost 2,000 years ago. According to tradition, Saint Mark the Evangelist was preaching Christianity in Alexandria, Egypt, not many years after the crucifixion of Jesus. The Christian Church in Alexandria regards him as its founder. A series of Christian Churches spread southward from Alexandria along the Nile River Valley, and by the 300s had reached Axum, the capital of an ancient Ethiopian kingdom. The Nile Valley Churches perished, except for the Egyptian Coptic Church, but Ethiopian Christianity survived and, isolated in a mountainous terrain, even withstood the influx of Muslims into East Africa in the 800s.

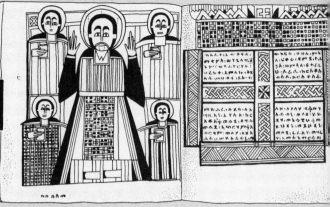

Illuminated manuscript
These pages from an illuminated manuscript of the Four Gospels were made in the 1600s. Christ and the Four Evangelists are shown on the left-hand page. The text is written in Geez, an ancient Ethiopian language, and was probably originally translated from Greek.

Cut from the living rock
Beta Ghiorghis, which means the "House of Saint George," is one of the eleven churches in Lalibela. It is cross shaped, and cut out of the solid rock. It is more than 40 ft (12 m) high. Legend says that St George himself supervised its construction, and the hoofprints of his horse are held to be still visible in the ditch around the church.

Lalibela

The heart of East African Christianity is Lalibela, which lies in rough country less than 100 miles (160 km) east of Lake Tana. Under its old name of Roha, it was the capital city of the Zagwe dynasty, which ruled in northern Ethiopia in the Middle Ages. Tradition has it that in the late 1300s a prince was born there and christened Lalibela, and the place is now named for him. When Lalibela became king, he set about constructing eleven churches in the town. The churches are cut into the solid, red volcanic rock in three groups. Four of the churches are huge blocks of stone cut and carved into buildings and set amid deep trenches. The other seven are more closely attached to the cliffs in which they are cut. A network of artificial caves and tunnels connects the churches, which are served by about a thousand priests and a community of nuns.

Despite the legend of Lalibela, some experts believe at least some of the churches were begun well before his time, possibly even before the arrival of Christianity in Ethiopia. One church is known to be older: it is the Church of Mekina Medahane Alem, which was built in the conventional way inside a vast cave 300 years before Lalibela. The town of Lalibela today is hardly more than a village, but it is a place of pilgrimage at Genna (Christmas) and Timkat (Epiphany – the revelation and baptism of Christ).

Christian art

Ethiopian Christian art is based on the cross, of which there are many elaborate designs. Craftsmen in the Axumite Kingdom made early crosses of gold or iron. When the center of government and Christianity moved to Lalibela, copper became the preferred metal. Later crosses, not made in Lalibela, are of wood or brass. The designs of crosses may have been copied from those of the Coptic Church of Egypt, with which the Ethiopian Church has links, and are of several types. Tall crosses are carried in processions; pilgrims carry crosses on

Pilgrim's prayers *(left)*
The pilgrim carries a carved wooden cross and a wooden staff. The staff represents the rod with which Moses struck a rock in the wilderness and brought forth water. He is reading from the most popular Ethiopian prayer book, the *Psalms of David*.

Ethiopian crosses *(above)*
Ethiopian crosses vary greatly in design but all are usually intricately worked. The cross shown is a processional cross and would be mounted on the end of a tall, wooden staff. Such crosses have been made in Ethiopia since the twelfth century. In Ethiopia, crosses are associated with the resurrection as well as the crucifixion of Christ.

staves on their shoulders; men and children wear neck crosses, while women wear theirs lower as pendants; priests have hand crosses for blessing the faithful. Cross symbols are also used in manuscripts as paragraph signs. Manuscript copies of the Gospels were made from the 1200s onward in Ethiopia, mostly on parchment and often richly decorated.

© DIAGRAM

East African Asians

Asians form a small but economically very important East African minority. Nairobi and Mombasa in Kenya have the largest East African Asian communities, but there are also significant concentrations in Dar es Salaam and Zanzibar in Tanzania, and a growing number are returning to Uganda after an absence of twenty years. The East African Asian population has reduced substantially since independence: in Kenya, the Asian population is around 50,000; in Tanzania, 30,000; and in Uganda, only a few thousand. Emigration has been substantial, with many East African Asians settling in Britain, Canada, or other countries.

History

There has been an Asian presence on the East African coast for many hundreds of years. The region has long been attractive to traders because of its excellent trading prospects. *Dhows* (cargo-carrying sailboats) plied between India, the Arabian Peninsula, and East Africa, supplying Indian-made textiles and iron goods in exchange for ivory, gold, slaves, and spices.

East African Asians timeline

1885–1900	Britain and Germany partition East Africa into colonies
1896–1902	Construction of the East Africa Railway – the "Lunatic Line"
1914	East African Indian National Congress formed
1961	Tanganyikan independence
1962	Ugandan independence
1963	Kenya and Zanzibar independent
1964	Tanganyika and Zanzibar unite to form Tanzania
1965	Each part of Tanzania is allowed only one political party
1966	Coup by Milton Obote in Uganda
1967	Arusha Declaration: Tanzania adopts socialism
1971	In Uganda, Col. Idi Amin Dada seizes power in a military coup; repressive regime installed
1972	Ugandan Asian community expelled by Amin; most go to Britain and others to Canada, Norway, or India
1979	Tanzanian forces and Ugandan rebels oust Amin
1981–1986	Ugandan civil war; rebels take power from government
1982	Failed military coup in Kenya results in widespread violence and looting, much of it targeting the Asian community
1985	Tanzania abandons socialism
1991	Kenya allows for multiparty politics. Uganda invites expelled Asians to return
1993	Anti-Asian attacks in Tanzania
1994	Nonparty elections held in Uganda as first step to restoring democracy
1995	Chaotic first multiparty elections held in Tanzania

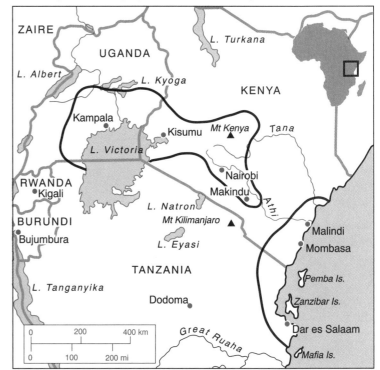

COLONIALISM The majority of the present-day Asian community dates back to the colonial era and the construction of the East Africa Railway (1896–1902) linking Mombasa with Uganda. Local African labor was either unavailable or was considered unreliable or hostile and so 32,000 laborers were recruited in India. Many of these workers died of tropical diseases, while others returned to India on completion of their contracts. About 7,000 Indians chose to settle in East Africa, however, while retaining close links with their home country. Although some Indians continued to work on the railways, most established themselves as merchants, initially catering to the needs of fellow Indians, but soon expanding their businesses to cater for the African population as well. Hearing of the business opportunities to be found in East Africa, Indian immigrants continued to arrive in the region into the 1920s, by which time Asians, through their trading activities, had done much to integrate even remote areas into the cash economy.

The East African Indian National Congress was formed in 1914 to represent the interests of the Asian community, in particular in demanding equal representation with Europeans on the Legislative Councils, equal economic opportunities (especially in relation to landownership in the highlands of Kenya), and in opposing segregation between Europeans and Asians. Their complaints were principally aimed at the European settler community, whom they far outnumbered. In marked contrast to the Indian community of South Africa and despite the urging of political leaders in India itself, East African Asians rarely took up common cause with the African population toward whom they tended to feel culturally superior.

RECENT EVENTS At independence, Asians were given a choice: they could become citizens of the country in which they lived or they could retain British nationality but without a right of residency in Britain. It was not an easy choice: adopting local citizenship implied loyalty to the new nation, but many Asians felt that their security in Africa was limited and believed that British nationality offered a measure of protection in the event of anti-Asian

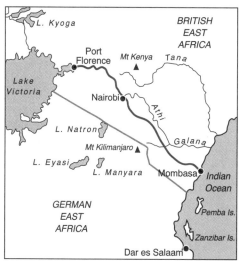

Lunatic Line
Built between 1896 and 1902, the "Lunatic Line"– as it was dubbed by its critics – was built to link Mombasa and Lake Victoria. The British intended to use it to transport troops. Over 30,000 Indian workers came from India to build the railway.

Hindu temple
This Hindu temple in Mombasa was built by volunteers between 1957 and 1960.

© DIAGRAM

Sikh temple
This Sikh temple at Makindu, like many others, offers free food and lodging to travelers. Visitors are restricted to one night's stay each.

Indian laborers
These workers are taking a rest from building the "Lunatic Line." The railway was built across hazardous and difficult terrain such as desert, the Great Rift Valley, and *tsetse fly*-infested land. Over 6,000 people were injured and 2,500 lives lost in the process.

hostilities. "Africanization" policies of the newly independent states resulted in Asians having to stop doing business in rural areas, but in the cities their skills and economic strength meant that they were not as easily replaced. Nevertheless, many found their shops nationalized or were pressured out of jobs, especially in government. In Kenya, the change happened slowly, thus avoiding disruption, but in Uganda the changes were sudden and brutal. In 1972, Uganda's dictator Idi Amin Dada expelled the entire Asian community of 80,000 from the country, distributing their businesses to his supporters. Although the expulsions were initially widely supported, they had a devastating effect on the Ugandan economy, from which the country is still recovering. In the 1990s, the current government has attempted to encourage the return of Ugandan Asians.

Language

Most East African Asians use Gujarati or Punjabi – languages spoken in western India – in their homes. Most also speak English, and many speak an African language, such as Swahili, as well.

Ways of life

Many East African Asians are in the retail trade, usually owning small shops. They also dominate – in Kenya, and to a lesser extent in Tanzania and Uganda – road transport, the textile and construction industries, hotels, and financial services. Some Asians have entered the profession of law, while others work as artisans or as clerks. In Uganda before 1972, Asians developed agricultural interests, especially in sugar; many have returned since 1991 and are again a major force in this sector.

Social structure

Under colonial rule, Asians occupied a middle rung on a three-tiered social and economic hierarchy that placed Europeans at the top and Africans at the bottom. Within their own community, East African Asians have largely retained the basic social structure developed in India. Religious divisions, including the maintenance of the Hindu *caste* structure, have resulted in a divided community. In general, the Asian community has isolated itself socially from mainstream society and has often been accused of economic exploitation and racism. Sensitive to such accusations, many Asians are active in charitable works, efforts that in the past would have been limited to supporting poorer members of the Asian community but are now extended to a wider population.

Culture and religion

East African Asians were (and still are) a highly visible minority, maintaining Indian styles of dress and cooking, although both have been subject to European and African influences.

RELIGION Most East African Asians are either Hindu or Muslim. Some of those whose families originated in the Punjab are Sikhs, and Zanzibar's few remaining *Parsees* (Indians originally descended from Persians) are *Zoroastrian*. Many of the Muslims are *Ismailis*, a subsect that has as its spiritual leader the Aga Khan, who maintains important business and philanthropic interests in the region, particularly in Kenya.

Street scene
This street scene in Nairobi, Kenya reflects the strong economic presence of Asians in Kenya. The Asians in East Africa have preserved much of their culture, such as their dress. Women still mostly wear Indian *saris* though many men have adopted Western styles of dress.

© DIAGRAM

Falasha

T he Falasha are mainly situated around the town of Gonder in the Ethiopian Highlands, which surround Lake Tana. They are not the only people in the area, and live scattered among many other ethnic groups in the Tigre and Gonder administrative regions. The Falasha number around 30,000 to 40,000 (roughly half of whom live in Israel).

The word Falasha is probably derived from an ancient Ethiopian word that means "exiles" or "strangers." The Falasha, who are Jewish, refer to themselves as "Beta Israel" ("House of Israel"). Although this community is known by the name of Falasha in international literature – without any derogatory intent – the Falasha themselves consider it an insulting name.

History

The Falasha themselves trace their ancestry to the Jewish bodyguard of Menelik I – the son of King Solomon and the Queen of Sheba – who, legend has it, founded the Ethiopian Solomonic dynasty. Indeed, Greek records mention Jews in Ethiopia as early as 200 BCE and by the 300s CE Judaism was widespread in the area. Other theories suggest that Egyptian or Palestinian Jews escaping religious purges over two thousand years ago spread Judaism to the area; that Jewish traders in the Red

Falasha timeline

200 BCE	Greek records mention Jews in Ethiopia
100 CE	Judaized peoples in Axumite Kingdom
300s	Falasha communities established in Gonder and Simien Mountains
c. 960	Falasha rebel against Axumite Kingdom
c. 1450	Falasha lands annexed by Ethiopian Empire
1500s	Falasha attempt to reassert independence
1616	Falasha massacred by Ethiopians
1790s	Existence of Falasha first known in West
1862	Aborted trek to Israel
1935– 1941	Italian invasion and occupation of Ethiopia
1961	Eritrean rebels begin armed struggle for independence
1972– 1974	Famine in Tigre and Wollo provinces; great civic unrest
1974	Military coup overthrows Haile Selassie in Ethiopia
1977	Maj. Mengistu Haile Miriam takes power in Ethiopia.
1980s	Severe *droughts* and famine
1984– 1985	7,000 refugee Falasha airlifted to Israel from Sudan
1991	Israel takes control of Addis Ababa airport to fly 14,000 Falasha out to escape civil war. Mengistu loses power
1993	Eritrea officially independent from Ethiopia
1996	Falasha demonstrate against discrimination in Israel

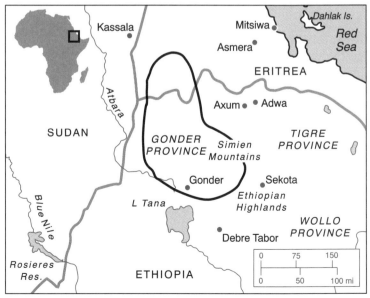

Sea converted Agaw people along the Ethiopian coast to Judaism; or even that the Falasha are the lost Old Testament tribe of Dan.

The Falasha were often influential in Ethiopia and had long periods of independence and power. Around 960, led by Queen Judith (or Esther), the Falasha rebelled against the Axumite Kingdom. Under the following Zagwe dynasty, they enjoyed great influence. Under the subsequent Christian Ethiopian Empire established in the thirteenth century, however, they were frequently persecuted. In the sixteenth century, the Emperor Sarsa Dengal (reigned 1563–97) waged a terrible war on the Falasha. His successor, Emperor Susneyos, broke their resistance in the massacre of 1616. Since then, the Falasha, who once numbered hundreds of thousands, have declined through persecution, conversion to Christianity, and emigration to a few thousand.

In the nineteenth century, European missionaries representing themselves as "white Falasha" told the Falasha that the promised Messiah had already lived in Jerusalem, in an attempt to convert them to Christianity. In 1862, many Falasha set out to walk to Israel to see for themselves. Decimated by disease and starvation, many died before the trek was abandoned at Axum.

RECENT EVENTS After years of debate, Israel declared that the Falasha had a right to Israeli citizenship in 1975. As the Ethiopian civil war took hold, the Falasha were among the many thousands of refugees who fled to camps in neighboring Sudan. From here, around 6,000 were able to get to the safety of Israel between 1979 and 1984. As the war worsened, a secret evacuation called "Operation Moses" took place: between 1984 and 1985 over 7,000 Falasha were airlifted to Israel from refugee camps in Sudan. In 1991, Israel took control of Addis Ababa airport to allow a further 14,000 Falasha to escape the civil war. Despite the great welcome they initially received, integration has been slow. In 1996, African Jews in Israel were demonstrating on the streets, protesting against being treated as second-class citizens.

Falasha priests
These two Falasha priests, or *cahenet*, are reading a prayer book in a *mesgid,* or *synagogue* (Jewish house of worship). Only priests are required to cover their heads. Weekday services are often accompanied by drums and cymbals.

Fasilidas' Castle
The castle of King Fasilida (reigned 1632–67) at Gonder, Ethiopia, which was built in the 1600s with the help of Falasha artisans. Deprived of the right to own land since 1616, many Falasha became craftworkers.

© DIAGRAM

49

Language

In the past, the Falasha spoke dialects of Agaw, which belongs to the Cushitic language group. Since the 1800s, however, the Falasha have adopted the languages of the people they live among and are now more likely to speak Tigrinya in the Tigre region or the national Ethiopian language of Amharic elsewhere. Furthermore, since the 1950s, Hebrew has been taught in Falasha schools.

Ways of life

AGRICULTURE Like their non-Jewish neighbors, most Falasha are farmers and herders. Their staple foods are dairy produce, millet, and fruit. The famine of the 1980s and the recent *droughts* (water shortages caused by periods of inadequate rainfall) have affected all farming communities in Ethiopia. The loss of many younger people to Israel has also left some communities without enough able workers. These factors have reduced many Falasha to poverty. During the period of socialism in Ethiopia (1974–91), the Marxist government adopted policies of *villagization* and reorganized many rural communities into collectives or relocated them elsewhere, sometimes with disastrous results, though some previously landless Falasha benefited.

SHELTER Falasha houses are circular in shape with stone, mud, or timber walls, and thatched roofs. The people live in their own villages, often nearby a river or spring – which in addition to normal uses provides for religious purification rituals – and usually set apart from nearby Christian settlements.

Pottery (above)
Falasha-made pottery is admired by many different people in Ethiopia. Much of this kind of work is carried out by Falasha women, who are also expert weavers of mats. Falasha men are said to be the best blacksmiths in Ethiopia.

Falasha village
Typical Falasha villages have circular houses with thatched roofs. This style of shelter is the same as that often lived in by other ethnic groups in Ethiopia.

Social organization

As in many Jewish communities, Falasha societies are organized around their religion. Each large village or group of small ones has a *kess* to lead the community; a *cahen* (plural *cahenet*) who conducts all the religious affairs of a community and instructs in the *Torah* (the first five books of the Old Testament); and a *bebtara* who helps the cahen by assisting with prayer services. The cahenet are provided for by the community and they are basically its leaders. Each family has its own cahen to give advice on religious matters. Disputes are settled by the village elders who are led by the cahenet.

Culture and religion

RELIGION The vast majority of Falasha are Jewish. They differ from other Jewish communities in that, until relatively recently, they were cut off from developments in Judaism elsewhere and did not know of the *Talmud* – a collection of writings and instructions on the Jewish way of life based on oral teachings from the time of Moses. Instead, their faith is based largely on the *Orit* (the Falasha name for the Torah). In many ways, however, the Falasha's form of Judaism is still very similar to that practiced elsewhere: they have equivalents of *rabbis* (Jewish religious leaders) called kess; the *Sabbath* (holy day of rest) is observed; boys undergo *circumcision*; all the festivals mentioned in the Orit are celebrated; and they adhere to the dietary laws as set out in the Orit.

Certain festivals are unique to the Falasha, such as *Sigd*, which celebrates the return of the exiles from Babylonia, and there are many fast days followed only by the cahenet. Other unique features include ritual immersion in water for purity and animal sacrifices on special occasions such as *Passover*, which commemorates the deliverance of ancient Hebrews from slavery in Egypt. Animal sacrifices are becoming less common though. Contact with other Jewish peoples has brought changes to the Falasha faith. Hebrew is increasingly used and many *mesgid* (houses of worship) now display the Star of David.

Prayer book
This prayer book is written in Geez, an ancient Ethiopian language little used today and generally understood only by the *cahenet* (priests). The congregation recite the prayers by heart facing Jerusalem. On the *Sabbath* (holy day of rest), the *Orit* (*Torah*) is usually read in the local language by the *cahen* and a sermon is given on matters of faith and on the commandments.

Ritual purity and impurity
Traditionally, Falasha women live in the village's "house of malediction" during their menstrual periods, during labor, and for a set period after the birth of a new baby. Before returning home, the women immerse themselves in water to become ritually pure. This practice is dying out, however, as the Falasha learn of different Jewish traditions.

© DIAGRAM

51

Ganda

The Ganda (or Baganda) people live in a large area of land to the north and west of Lake Victoria in Uganda. The islands in Lake Victoria are inhabited by a people known as the Basese, who are part of the Ganda. There are over three million Ganda people, who form the largest single ethnic grouping in Uganda.

History

There is plenty of information on Ganda history as each *clan* (extended families who share an ancestor or ancestors) kept its own oral history while court historians preserved royal accounts. The Ganda are descendants of Bantu-speaking people who migrated to East Africa from Central Africa around 1000. Some settled on the northwest corner of Lake Victoria around the Kyadondo region. By the 1300s, this was the heart of a small state, the Buganda Kingdom.

The head of state was the *kabaka* whose role initially was one of arbiter rather than ruler. His power was limited by that of the *batakas*, or clan heads. During the eighteenth century, however, successive kabakas skillfully

Ganda timeline

c. 1000	Bantu-speakers migrate from Central to East Africa; Ganda settle around northwest Lake Victoria
1500s	Buganda Kingdom expands
c. 1650	Bataka mutiny against authoritarian kabaka
1700s	Kabakas increase power
1800s	Buganda evolves into centralized monarchy
1894	British *protectorate* (colony) over Buganda formed
1900	Buganda is made a semiautonomous province of British Uganda Protectorate
1921	Bataka Association formed to grievances over land allocation under British rule
1955	Kabaka made a constitutional monarch and Lukiko becomes a mainly elected body
1962	Uganda gains independence
1963	Kabaka Mutesa II made first president (nonexecutive) of Ugandan Republic
1966	Coup led by prime minister Milton Obote; Mutesa II flees; Obote becomes president
1967	Buganda Kingdom abolished
1971	Col. Idi Amin Dada seizes power in a military coup; he installs repressive regime
1979	Tanzanian forces and Ugandan rebels oust Amin
1981– 1986	Ugandan civil war; rebels led by Yoweri Museveni win power
1993	Bugandan monarchy restored; Ronald Mutebi is kabaka
1994	Nonparty elections held as first step to restoring democracy
1996	Reports of rebel activites in Uganda

Bugandan hospitality
In the 1860s, the British explorers John Hanning Speke and James Augustus Grant visited Buganda in their search for the source of the Nile. This picture of the event shows them at the palace of Kabaka Mutesa I. Speke and his men were held as virtual prisoners for six months before Mutesa allowed them to leave.

increased their powers at the expense of the batakas. Buganda eventually became a centralized monarchy with the kabaka acting as king.

Despite clashes with the dominant, northerly kingdom of Bunyoro, Buganda increased in size from the sixteenth century onward. By 1870, Buganda was a wealthy and influential nation state with a highly organized system of government led by the kabaka with help from his *Lukiko* (council of ministers). A currency of cowrie shells, their value denoted by the holes drilled in the shells so that they could be suspended on strings, was in use. The Basese provided the kabakas with a useful naval capacity, and could sometimes muster fleets of as many as a hundred vessels, each crewed by up to thirty men. This growing economic, political, and military strength had an effect on neighboring areas, particularly on Bunyoro. Buganda supplanted Bunyoro in importance and dominated the region throughout the nineteenth century, helped by several factors. Prime among these was the absence of a Ganda *caste* system, their military superiority, and their talent for administration.

In 1900, the Buganda Agreement between the British and Bugandan regents (the reigning kabaka was still a boy at the time) made the kingdom a province of the Uganda Protectorate. Its territory was reorganized and numerous counties and parishes were created, each with its own head. In 1955, a second Buganda Agreement

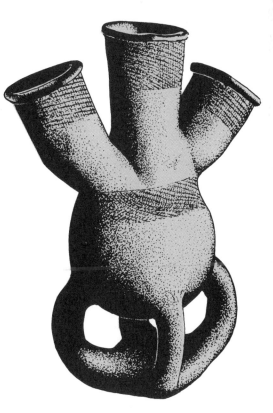

Medicine pot
This large pottery vessel would have once been used for administering medicine, often mixed with beer. Royalty drank from the central spout; ordinary people from the spout on the right; and *batakas* (chiefs) from the left.

© DIAGRAM

53

made the kabaka a constitutional monarch and the Lukiko became an elected body. As the identity of the wider state of Uganda began to emerge, the solidarity of the Ganda became a block to national unity. Uganda finally became an independent republic in 1962 with Milton Obote as prime minister. Kabaka Mutesa II was made the first president the following year. He was arrested and dismissed in 1966, however, by Obote – an act that led to widespread rioting in Buganda. In 1967, traditional kingdoms were abolished in Uganda. In 1993, however, the Bugandan monarchy, among others, was restored but with a purely ceremonial and cultural role. Although the monarchy has no real political power, the very fact that it has been restored is, in part, due to its political influence.

Language

The language the Ganda speak is Ganda (or Luganda). This is one of the interlacustrine (between the lakes) branches of the Bantu language group. The Basese speak a dialect of Luganda.

Ways of life

AGRICULTURE The Ganda are mostly agriculturalists. Much of the southern part of their territory is fertile. Because the terrain here is on average more than 3,000 ft (900 m) above sea level, the climate is usually warm but seldom very hot. Rainfall is evenly distributed throughout the year. The staple crops are bananas and plantains, but in modern times the Ganda produce many cash crops. Coffee is particularly successful and, indeed, even before it was cultivated grew in the wild. Other cash crops grown by the Ganda are cotton, sugar cane, corn, rice, and tea. The north and northeast parts of the land are less fertile. Most of the northern border is a region known as a dry zone, and in the northeast are the Kyoga Swamps around Lake Kyoga.

INDUSTRY The Ganda are famous in the region for their basket-making, and many of their village houses were built by weaving long reeds. The kabaka's own residence

Luzira Head
Discovered in 1929, the so-called "Luzira Head" is actually two pieces of terra-cotta pottery – a head and a body. Little is known about them; they date from any time between c. 1000 to c. 750 and may have been parts of separate pieces that have since been lost. Luzira was once the site of an ancient shrine, the guardians of which were royal bark-cloth makers. It is usually assumed that the pieces had some religious purpose related to this shrine.

Mutesa I's tomb
The tall tomb of this Bugandan king is made from long, woven reeds. Mutesa I ruled over Buganda from 1852 until his death in 1884. The kingdom reached its height during this period and, by then, the position of *kabaka* was one of absolute monarch. Mutesa is renowned for being a particularly cruel ruler. He was succeeded by his son who was young and inexperienced at a time when Buganda needed a decisive ruler.

had such walls in excess of 15 ft (5 m) in height. The Ganda were also able to smelt iron using charcoal, building their furnaces with slabs cut from the sides of termite hills. The Basese are renowned fishermen and boat builders.

Social structure

At the time of the Bugandan Kingdom, prestige, wealth, and status could be achieved through military service or service at the court of the kabaka. Talented and ambitious people could, therefore, move upward in Bugandan society. This tradition of advancement through patronage and service is harder to achieve in modern Ugandan society, where education is the key. Nevertheless, the Ganda have an established "middle class" and tend to be among the more prosperous members of Ugandan society. Also, the Ganda people dominate the country's civil service.

Historically, the kabaka guaranteed the rights of all his subjects wherever they resided, land was plentiful, and people were not dependent on their neighbors and families for their status and security. The Ganda argue that this is why it is now customary for men to move from one village to another every few years and not to settle down until middle age. Consequently, Ganda families are largely self-contained units and this is reflected in the villages, which are not particularly close knit.

Culture and religion

RELIGION In recent years, many Ganda have become either Muslim or Christian. They still retain, however, their own systems of belief. The Ganda have one of the most elaborate religions in Africa involving various gods and spirits who are associated with ideas or places such as the forest, a river, or even a particular tree. In the past, each had its own temple, priest, or medium. The most influential of these deities is the great god, *Mukasa*. The brother of Mukasa, the kindly god, is *Kibuka* – the war god. *Kintu* is believed to have been the first man and ancestor; *Nambi*, daughter of the King of Heaven, became his wife and brought her brother, Death, down to earth.

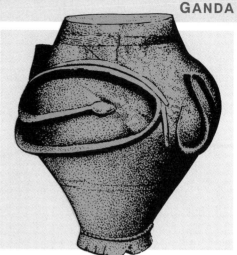

Ceremonial drum
This ancient drum was beaten by the *kabaka*.

Kabaka Mutesa II
Kabaka Mutesa II was the first president of the Republic of Uganda and, until 1993, the last king of the Bugandan dynasty. He ruled over Buganda from 1939 to 1967, but the kingdom was never fully independent. It was a province of the British Uganda Protectorate, with some autonomy, and the kabaka kept his status, if not his power, up to 1962. The Bugandan monarchy was restored in 1993 with a purely ceremonial role.

© DIAGRAM

Coffee, tea, and other cash crops

Agriculture dominates East African economies. The region has been integrated into the world market for centuries. European colonial penetration of the region in the late nineteenth century, however, established the large-scale production of export-oriented crops, especially sisal (a fiber crop), cotton, tobacco, tea, and coffee. Much of the best land was taken by colonialists to develop plantations, forcing dispossessed Africans to work less desirable land or take up employment as laborers, often on a seasonal basis. Others found it necessary to produce cash crops as a means of paying taxes and school fees.

Coffee

Coffee originates in Ethiopia, with commercial production dating back a thousand years. The crop spread across the Red Sea to Yemen and eventually to other parts of the world. Arabica coffee is a major Ethiopian export, but production is on a relatively small scale. Cultivated and wild bushes are stripped of both ripe and unripe beans and a lot of the coffee produced is low quality and unsuitable for export. Small quantities of good-quality coffee are produced that are highly rated by European consumers.

Coffee is also a major cash crop in Kenya, Rwanda, Burundi, and Uganda, which has its own native coffee variety (Robusta). There have never been coffee plantations in Uganda and production is mainly by peasant farmers who, since about 1950, have produced coffee as their main cash crop instead of cotton. There have been periods when Ugandan farmers have suffered from their dependency on coffee, which is subject to considerable price swings and changes in government purchasing policies.

Tea

In East Africa, small-scale tea production for the local market began in 1924. After World War II, British tea companies feared that their south Asian production base would be nationalized when India

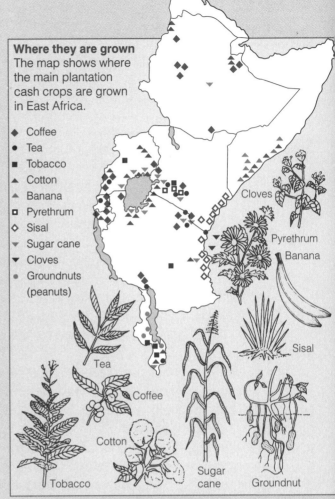

Where they are grown
The map shows where the main plantation cash crops are grown in East Africa.

- ◆ Coffee
- ● Tea
- ■ Tobacco
- ▲ Cotton
- ▲ Banana
- ◻ Pyrethrum
- ◇ Sisal
- ▽ Sugar cane
- ▼ Cloves
- ● Groundnuts (peanuts)

Cloves

Pyrethrum

Banana

Sisal

Tea

Coffee

Cotton

Sugar cane

Groundnut

Tobacco

and Sri Lanka became independent. So they concentrated on expanding production in Africa. The climate and soils of Tanzania, Malawi, and the Kenyan Highlands are ideal for tea production and there are plenty of available workers for this labor-intensive industry. Today, India is Kenya's main tea producing rival. Kenyan labor is more expensive than Indian and, as a result, Kenyan producers are more capital intensive and more dependent on machinery, fertilizers, and pesticides than labor.

Other cash crops

Tobacco has long been widely produced in East Africa. During the 1980s, it became an important crop for Ugandan smallholders, with some negative environmental consequences. Wood is required to fire the furnaces used for curing tobacco; this has led to widespread deforestation. In turn, deforestation has caused streams and rivers to dry up, forcing women and children to walk farther to collect water. In addition, the loss of forest cover has resulted in the fertile topsoil being washed away.

Ethiopia exports a considerable amount of qat (a mild stimulant) to southwest Asia. Also, until the country lost control of the main area of production along the Sudanese border – because of the war in Sudan – Ethiopia was a significant sesame seed producer. Bananas are the most important export crop of Somalia. When Italy, the main customer, levied a tax on Somalian bananas in the 1980s, the economy was badly affected – this tax has since been abolished. Other important crops grown in East Africa include cotton, cloves, and sugar cane.

New cash crops

In recent years, East African farmers have turned to new types of cash crop production, keen to decrease their dependency on a single earner. Pyrethrum is produced by some East African countries such as Kenya and Rwanda. It is an insecticide ingredient

Drying coffee
These coffee beans are drying on racks in Kenya. The ripe, red berries are picked between October and December, and left exposed to the Sun on such racks for around ten days. The beans can then be removed from their husks.

made from chrysanthemums. In Kenya, flowers, fruit, and vegetables (such as green beans and strawberries) produced for the European winter market are now an important source of income for small farmers. The purchasing criteria, however, are extremely rigorous and farmers are subject to the high costs of approved seeds or cuttings, pesticides, and fertilizers, which are either imported or made locally by international chemical giants. The use of pesticides has become an important issue as most spraying is done without protective clothing, and this has serious effects on the farmers' health.

In recent decades, attempts have been made to establish more processing plants such as factories to wash coffee and distilleries to produce clove oil. This is beneficial as more revenue can be earned from the export of processed goods than of raw materials.

Kenyan tea pickers
The precolonial Kenyan tea industry was based on large, British-owned plantations. Land reform programs have since transferred most production to small-holdings. Tea estates are now mostly Kenyan-owned, self-contained communities in which conditions vary greatly according to the plantation owners.

Hutu and Tutsi

T he Hutu (or Bahutu) and the Tutsi (or Watutsi) are two ethnic groups that make up the majority populations of Burundi and Rwanda. In the past, the Hutu have formed as much as ninety percent of the population of both countries, and the Tutsi nine percent. Minority groups, mostly Twa people, form the rest. Since the fighting that began more than three years ago, however, a great number of Hutu, and some Tutsi, have fled as refugees to neighboring countries – in particular Zaire – severely reducing the numbers of Hutu remaining in their homelands.

Although they are generally considered to be distinct ethnic groups, the history and lives of the Hutu and Tutsi are so intertwined that they are described together here.

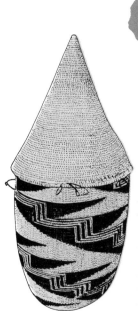

Basketwork
Ornamental baskets and basket trays were made by Tutsi women who were members of the aristocracy. Elegantly patterned and carefully worked, the baskets required the amount of time that only members of a leisured class would have.

History

RUANDA–URUNDI The Twa, who are largely *hunter-gatherers* and potters, were probably the first peoples of Burundi and Rwanda. The Hutu came from the west (modern Zaire) a very long time ago. About 600 years ago, the Tutsi moved in from Ethiopia. They soon dominated the Hutu, who became virtual slaves. The Tutsi founded two kingdoms, known as Ruanda and Urundi. Ruanda was especially powerful. Each kingdom was ruled by a Tutsi king, the *mwami*. The Tutsi continued to dominate both countries, even after Europeans established colonial rule there. Germany made Ruanda-Urundi a joint territory as part of German East Africa in 1890, but did not exercise much authority over it. Belgium occupied Ruanda-Urundi during World War I, and from 1924 administered it under trust from the League of Nations (later the United Nations).

INDEPENDENCE In 1962, the two countries became independent. Urundi, now called Burundi, remained a monarchy under its Tutsi mwami, Mwambutsa IV. Conflict between the Hutu and the Tutsi followed. In 1966 the prime minister, Michel Micombero, overthrew the monarchy and declared a republic. An unsuccessful Hutu revolt in 1972 resulted in heavy loss of life, mostly among the Hutu. The Tutsi remained in control of the country, despite outbreaks of ethnic warfare that killed

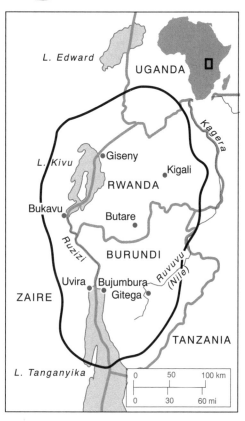

tens of thousands of people, especially in 1993. In that year, Burundi's first ever Hutu president was killed, probably in an attempted coup, and over 50,000 people died in the ensuing violence.

Rwanda became an independent republic, with a predominantly Hutu government, in 1962. There was heavy fighting between Hutu and Tutsi in the years before and immediately after independence. The Tutsi sustained the most casualties, and thousands fled to other countries, where many later settled and some became rebels.

RECENT EVENTS Tutsi rebels went on to form the Rwandan Patriotic Front, and although a peace accord between them and the Hutu government was signed in 1993 after three years of conflict, large-scale violence broke out again in 1994, after a plane carrying the presidents of both countries crashed near Rwanda's capital, Kigali, having possibly been hit by gunfire or a rocket. A series of vicious riots and massacres followed, mainly of the Tutsi, resulting in hundreds of thousands dead and more than a million people fleeing to refugee camps in Zaire and other neighboring countries. In 1996, the violence spread to Burundi.

Language

Both Hutu and Tutsi speak a Bantu language, called Rundi (or Kirundi) in Burundi and Rwanda (or Kinyarwanda) in Rwanda. This was originally a Hutu language, which the Tutsi have since adopted.

Ways of life

HUTU Although many Hutu live and work in Rwandan or Burundi towns and cities, the vast majority are farmers. Among them, the Hutu of both sexes have long tilled the soil and grown crops. The men also looked after cattle, often under the supervision of a Tutsi overseer.

The Hutu live in small fenced *compounds,* each containing several reed and grass structures. One is a kitchen, one a bedroom and sitting room, and a third is for storage. A fourth, among those Hutu who are not Christians, is for the ancestral spirits. Others serve as *granaries* (storehouses for grain). A group of about

Hutu/Tutsi timeline	
upto 1500s	Hutu move from present-day Zaire into present area
1500s	Tutsi herders migrate into Hutu and Twa lands from northeast
c. 1550s	Tutsi found kingdom of Ruanda
1600s	Tutsi kingdom in Urundi
1897	Urundi under German colonial rule
1899	Ruanda's expansion ended by Germans
1916–1917	Ruanda-Urundi occupied by Belgium
1959	Hutu subjects overthrow Ruandan monarchy
1962	Ruanda wins independence and becomes Rwanda. Urundi wins independence under Tutsi monarchy and becomes Burundi
1972	Burundi Hutu revolt against Tutsi elite; over 100,000 Hutu killed in retaliation. Tension between Hutu and Tutsi in Rwanda precedes military coup
1980	Tanzania grants citizenship to 36,000 (mainly Tutsi) Rwandan refugees
1988	80,000 Hutu refugees from Burundi enter Rwanda
1990	10,000 Tutsi-dominated guerrillas invade Rwanda; civil war follows
1992	In Rwanda, 300 Tutsi assassinated; 15,000 forcibly relocated
1993	In Burundi, 50,000 die in ethnic war. Peace agreed in Rwanda between Tutsi rebels and Hutu government
1994	Hutu presidents of Rwanda and Burundi die in plane crash, probably assassinated; large-scale massacres in Rwanda and massive refugee crisis follow
1995	Fighting between Hutu and Tutsi intensifies in Burundi
1996	Burundi president toppled in coup. War crimes tribunal begins work (in Tanzania)

© DIAGRAM

A Tutsi dancer
This Tutsi dancer wears a leopardskin cloak and a headdress and carries a spear. Most dancers now carry javelinlike wands rather than spears. The headdress accentuates the rhythmic movements of the dance.

A Tutsi woman
This aristocratic woman is a Tutsi chief's wife. The Tutsi often cultivate an arisotcratic bearing that, historically, helped to separate them from their Hutu subjects more than any real physical difference. Indeed, some regard the diference between Hutu and Tutsi to be one of class, not ethnicity.

twenty compounds makes up a Hutu village.

For years many Hutu, regarded as second-class citizens, have had a largely subsistence diet. It is based on cereals, beans, peas, bananas, and sweet potatoes, with a little goat flesh. When they can, the Hutu eat two solid meals a day of porridge and sweet potatoes. Many dislike sheep flesh and fish. The Hutu make two kinds of beer, one from bananas and one from cassava.

TUTSI In the past, the Tutsi regarded themselves as the only people who ought to own and tend cattle. They expected the Hutu to work for them and do all the dirty jobs such as farming. Today, they work the land like the Hutu, and no longer have exclusive rights to own cattle. Coffee is an important cash crop for both groups, followed by tea. Cattle, goats, and sheep are the main livestock. The Tutsi diet is different from that of the Hutu and in the past was based on curdled milk and butter. A few Tutsi claimed to eat nothing else, but most had one solid meal a day of bananas and beans. Banana beer and mead, made from honey, are drunk.

Social structure

The Tutsi have long considered themselves superior to the Hutu, and until recent years have exclusively formed the ruling classes. The Tutsi, however, allowed some Hutu men to rise to high office. For a long time the Tutsi were the fighting soldiers in any army, with the Hutu providing the supporting services such as servants and carriers. Until modern times, members of each Hutu village or group were "clients" subservient to a Tutsi "patron." Clients were given a cow and in exchange provided beer and agricultural goods to the patron, who protected them against exactions by other Tutsi. This system was called *ubuhake*.

MARRIAGE The Hutu often marry young (around seventeen for boys, the girls around puberty), usually with local partners. The bridegroom's father has to pay the *bridewealth,* a gift of cows, goats, and beer given to the bride's family and generally regarded as a token of respect. Both husband and wife are allowed sexual freedom.

Hutu men may have more than one wife, each with her own compound. Children are prized, partly because they mean extra pairs of hands to share the work. The Hutu regard twins of different sexes as bad luck. The man owns the labor of his wife or wives and his children if unmarried. When he dies, the eldest son of his first wife generally succeeds him. Marriage between Hutu and Tutsi sometimes takes place.

Tutsi marriage customs were not unlike those of the Hutu, the groom having to pay the bridewealth. In general, the Tutsi marry among themselves, but they allow some Hutu men to marry Tutsi women. Such a marriage makes the children automatically Tutsi.

Culture and religion

RELIGION Today, more than half the Hutu and Tutsi in both Rwanda and Burundi are Christians, mostly Roman Catholics. Others follow their original beliefs, perhaps in conjunction with Christianity, worshipping a benevolent god called *Imana*, and acknowledging witches, sorcerers, and the ghosts of the dead. The Hutu take a keen interest in family relationships and remember ancestors, to whom they show respect and make offerings to at the family ancestral shrines, for as many as six generations back.

DRESS In recent years, traditional forms of Hutu dress have tended to die out in favor of "Western" styles and imported fabrics: shorts and shirts for men; skirts and tops for women. Tutsi dress today is also largely "Western" style. Traditional dress is seen now mostly among the Tutsi dancers, who perform largely at ceremonial events.

CRAFTS Hutu crafts include basket-making, carving, and blacksmithing. Both the Tutsi and Hutu make some pottery, but they usually rely on trading agricultural produce for pots with the Twa or purchase plastic containers. The Tutsi are especially skilled in weaving baskets and in beadwork and also make ornamental screens.

Hutu knife
This knife has a wooden handle and a metal blade shaped into a flat hook. Such knives are widespread throughout East and Central Africa. They are used mainly by women to knock fruit from trees, but can also serve as weapons if necessary.

Igikubge
A headdress called an *igikubge* is worn by some Tutsi women of royal ancestry. A leaf is made into a band and decorated with beadwork, inlcuding beaded tassels that hang over the wearer's face.

War orphan
This child is a casualty of the 1990s conflict in Rwanda, and more recently Burundi, between the Tutsi-dominated rebels and the majority Hutu people. Large numbers of Hutu refugees fled to neighboring countries while many Tutsi families found themselves the victims of retaliation.

© DIAGRAM

61

Karamojong

Karamojong is the collective name given to several closely related ethnic groups who live in Karamoja, a semiarid plateau in northeast Uganda on the border with Kenya. The Turkana, who live across the border in Kenya, are sometimes considered one of the Karamojong. The other groups are the Dodoth, Jie, Bokora, Matheniko, and Pian. The Karamojong total a few hundred thousand: the exact number is not known.

History

The Karamojong moved into Karamoja hundreds of years ago. The groups are all Nilotic in origin – some of their ancestors originally came from the Nile River region in present-day southern Sudan. The Karamojong have suffered from a number of severe *droughts* (periods of inadequate rainfall) and famines since the early 1700s. In the late nineteenth century, drought was accompanied by epidemics, both cattle and human, that devastated the herds and led to the present widespread dispersal of the Karamojong people. Until fairly recently, the Karamojong were isolated and were thus able to maintain their own ways of life, including the cattle rustling that was a major occupation. Raids by one Karamojong group to steal the cattle of another were carried out by warriors armed with

Karamojong timeline

1000s–1500s	Karamojong ancestors migrate toward Mount Elgon
1600s	Teso group breaks away
1700s	Karamojong settle north of Mount Elgon
1706–1733	Period of *drought* and famine known as the "Nyamdere"
1894	An epidemic of cattle diseases decimates Karamojong herds and disperses the people
1900	British-ruled Uganda Protectorate established
1916	British control Karamoja region
1962	Uganda wins independence; Milton Obote is prime minister
1966	Political coup against his opponents led by Obote, who becomes president
1970	Karamojong refuse to join Ugandan army
1971	Col. Idi Amin Dada seizes power in military coup; during his rule, 30,000 Karamojong are executed "for being too primitive"
1979	Tanzanian forces and Ugandan rebels oust Amin; Karamojong arm themselves from barracks of routed Amin troops
1980	Obote elected president
1980s	Armed cattle rustlers disrupt life in Karamojong province
1981–1986	Ugandan civil war; rebels led by Yoweri Museveni win power and install military government
1994	Nonparty elections held as first step to restoring democracy
1995	Karamojong leaders hold "Peace Forum" with officials to resolve arms crisis

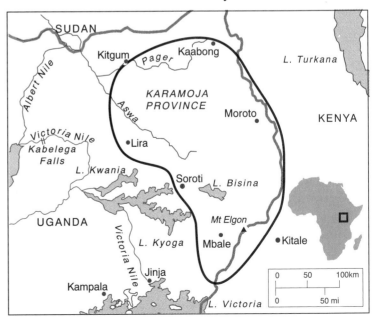

spears, who followed various rules of engagement when fighting with another group – in order to limit unnecessary damage and prevent undue conflict. But the British, who administered Karamojong territory earlier this century, tried to ban the ownership and use of spears. At one time, the administration decided to provide steel plows to encourage the Karamojong to adopt farming and settle in one place – therefore making them easier to control, govern, and tax. The Karamojong accepted them gratefully, but blacksmiths reworked many of the plowshares into new spear blades. This is an example of British attempts to "modernize" (though actually to control) the Karamojong.

RECENT EVENTS Since independence in the 1960s, attempts at control disguised as "modernization" have continued, sometimes by force, and they were especially harsh during the reign of the brutal dictator Idi Amin Dada (1971–9), during which 30,000 Karamojong were executed allegedly "for being too primitve." When Amin's troops fled the country in 1979, the Karamojong armed themselves from the abandoned army barracks. The abundance of guns, mostly automatic rifles, disrupted life in Karamoja province in the 1980s, greatly increasing the crime rate. A group of Karamojong elders took matters into their own hands and attempted to curb the rising lawlessness, at first rather brutally. In 1995, government officials, Karamojong elders, and other concerned parties attended a "Peace Forum" to resolve the problem. It was decided to register all weapons in Karamoja and turn the armed men into government-paid, local police forces responsible for policing their own communities under guidance from the elders.

Language

The Karamojong language is a Nilotic language.

Ways of life

PASTORALISM Most Karamojong are cattle-herding *pastoralists,* who also keep sheep and goats. They also grow crops, which include millet, corn, *groundnuts* (peanuts), gourds, and marrows. Rainfall is unpredictable,

Stool
This low wooden stool was crafted by a Karamojong artisan and was probably intended to be used by a man.

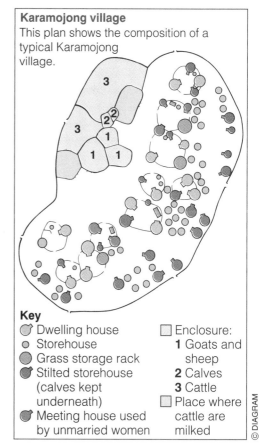

Karamojong village
This plan shows the composition of a typical Karamojong village.

Key
- Dwelling house
- Storehouse
- Grass storage rack
- Stilted storehouse (calves kept underneath)
- Meeting house used by unmarried women
- Enclosure:
  - **1** Goats and sheep
  - **2** Calves
  - **3** Cattle
- Place where cattle are milked

© DIAGRAM

Women builders
Karamojong women build their own homes. They weave together poles and straw to make a framework, then plaster the walls with mud. Then, they cover each structure with a stepped roof of thatch.

and the crops frequently fail. During the wet season, from late March to September, water is plentiful. During the dry season, from October to early March, water is scarce in the east, and the men must move the cattle to stock camps in the west, near permanent water sources.

DIVISION OF LABOR Among the Karamojong ways of life differ greatly between the sexes. Men between the ages of fifteen and thirty spend most of their time with the herds. They move with the cattle from one grazing ground to another. In the dry season, they may be many miles from home, living in makeshift homes if any.

Karamojong women spend most of their time in or near the stockade. They are expected to do all the hard work around the homestead, including collecting firewood, fetching water, and growing and tending the crops. Day begins with milking the cows and goats. The women shake the milk in gourds until it separates into curds and whey. They mix the whey with grain to make porridge, or drink it as it is. Curds can be used as body lotion. Each woman has her own patch of ground near the settlement. The main crop is sorghum, next to which comes millet. These cereals not only provide grain – which the women grind laboriously between two stones – but are also fermented to make beer. Each woman builds her own home, plus one used as a kitchen, another for her children, and several on stilts that serve as storehouses.

Social structure

Within Karamojong society there are several systems of classification, most based on different celebrations. One system is the hereditary *clan* (several extended families related by a common

Hairdo extraordinary
Karamojong warriors used to spend a lot of time on elaborate hairstyles, created by a skilled barber. Young warriors had their hair bonded with grease and made into a huge bunlike pile on the back of the head. Older warriors who had passed an initiation ceremony had a more elaborate bun reinforced with colored clay and painted. These styles took many days to complete.

ancestor or ancestors) each of which has its own cattle brand. The Karamojong are also organized by geography into *ngitela*, areas occupied by people who celebrate social and religious events together. Another is the system of *ngikenoi*, which means "fireplaces with three stones." These are subsections of Karamojong society whose members gather for certain ceremonies. Festivities related to the seasons and the harvest are celebrated by members of an *ekitela*. The most common of these festivities is known as an *aperit*, which means "where people sleep." It is literally a sleep over by elders who gather at a place to eat, drink, and share a pipe.

AGE-SETS *Age-sets*, groups of men of the same generation, are important elements of Karamojong society. Once they have passed through the male initiation ceremony called the *asapan* (any time between the ages of eighteen and forty), a man can participate in the assemblies by which many decisions are made. Authority rests with the elders of a group, who make up the most senior age-set.

Women also go through an initiation, called an *akiwor* ("giving a name for the first time"). This bestows a certain measure of respect on a woman.

MARRIAGE It is ususal for Karamojong couples to have long engagements: five years is not uncommon. The reason is the high *bridewealth* a groom has to pay to the bride's family, which may be as much as fifty heads of cattle and fifty goats. This is not considered to be a payment for his wife, but a token of respect to the family or compensation for the loss of a working member.

Culture and religion

RELIGION The Karamojong worship one all-powerful god, who they call *Akuj*. They pray to Akuj regularly, with senior members of the settlement acting as priests.

CATTLE The Karamojong regard their cattle as wealth and as objects to be respected. Each boy has an ox named for him, and his attachment to it continues into adulthood. A man takes great care of his name-ox, and may even be heard singing to it. If he should die, the ox is slaughtered. If the ox dies, the name-sharer is distraught.

Water carriers
These young girls are fetching water in large clay pots carried on their heads. This is a daily chore for women and children. They are wearing old-fashioned clothes made from animal skins rather than cloth, which is more often worn nowadays.

Headrest
A headrest was essential for a man to maintain his elaborate hairstyle while sleeping. There are various designs for the headrests; some have two legs, others three.

© DIAGRAM

65

Kikuyu

T he Kikuyu, sometimes called the Gikuyu, are the largest ethnic group in Kenya. They total more than 4.5 million and they form around twenty percent of the country's population. Their homeland is sometimes known as Kikuyuland, a highland plateau – part of the lush Great Rift Valley at the foot of Mount Kenya – furrowed by rivers flowing in deep gorges between high ridges. This area has a pleasant climate, with reliable rainfall and moderate temperatures.

History

The origins of the Kikuyu are obscure. Ethnologists believe they came to Kenya from the north and west and began to settle in Kikuyuland in the 1500s. They were originally hunters and *nomadic pastoralists* (livestock raisers who migrated with their herds). Their expansion in Kenya continued until the 1800s. They were generally on good terms with their neighbors the Maasai, with whom they traded agricultural produce for hides and livestock.

COLONIALISM The Kikuyu's settled existence was radically disturbed by the European "scramble" for African colonies, which began in the 1880s. A private British company began to set up trading facilities on the coast. In 1895, the British government took over and set up the colony of British East Africa, later called Kenya. The British built a railroad from the coast to the shores of

Kikuyu timeline

1400s on	Eastern Bantu-speakers migrate into region of present-day Kenya
1500s–1600s	Kikuyu settle southeast of Mount Kenya
1700s–1800s	Period of expansion and migration
1895	British take control of Kenya
1920	Kikuyu Central Association (precursor to KANU) formed to fight oppression by British
1934	British Commission extends Kikuyuland in Nairobi region as compensation for land taken earlier for settlers
1952–1956	Terrorism by Mau Mau, a Kikuyu anticolonial society; 50,000 Kikuyu confined in detention camps
1963	Kenya wins independence; Jomo Kenyatta becomes first prime minister and later president
1978	Kenyatta dies; Daniel arap Moi becomes president
1986	"Mwakenya Conspiracy"– mainly Kikuyu political opposition suppressed
1991	Kenya allows for multiparty politics
1992	Moi reelected in democratic elections contested as fraudulent by opposition
1993–1994	Kikuyu and Maasai clash in Great Rift Valley area. Many Kikuyu in Rift Valley lose land to Kalenjins; government accused of ethnic cleansing

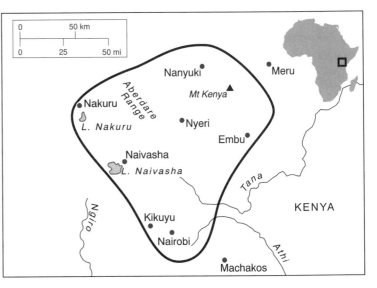

Lake Victoria, set up a base at Nairobi, and began to settle in the heart of Kikuyuland. They took over land from the Kikuyu, who were confined to a small reserve, unable to farm on the inadequate land. Many Kikuyu were forced to leave the land and work for the European settlers, or in the factories that sprang up in Nairobi. British officials ruled the colony, and the Kikuyu became third-class citizens (Asians were the middle class). During World War I, many Kikuyu men worked as "carriers" for the British troops. In 1920, the Kikuyu Central Association was established, partly as a response to the discrimination experienced by Kikuyu veterans. In the 1940s, along with other ethnic groups, they began to organize opposition to the colonial power. Many Kikuyu men also served in World War II, fighting against the Germans, and again after the war they were bitter about their treatment. When progress toward independence seemed to be too slow, some Kikuyu organized a society, Mau Mau, which began to commit acts of anticolonial terrorism. Fighting between the Kikuyu and loyalist and British troops continued until 1956, during which 13,000 Africans – mostly Kikuyu – were killed.

INDEPENDENCE Independence was granted in 1963. In elections held that year, the Kenya African National Union (KANU) secured a majority in parliament. KANU was composed largely of Kikuyu and was led by Jomo Kenyatta, the country's first president in 1964 – a position he held until his death in 1978. Other ethnic groups formed opposition parties, but the Kikuyu, who were among the best educated people in Kenya, held many of the top posts in government and the civil service. After Kenyatta's death and the succession of vice-president Daniel arap Moi as president, political activity was tightly restricted. Discontent with the one-

Valley view
In the Great Rift Valley, the historic, round, thatched-roof huts of the Kikuyu have largely been replaced by square and rectangular homes with iron roofs.

Mau Mau detention camp prisoners
Prisoners – alleged supporters of the Mau Mau rebellion – were kept in detention camps. Around 80,000 Kikuyu were imprisoned by British security forces in an attempt to crush the Mau Mau rebellion in the early 1950s. Jomo Kenyatta was one of those imprisoned; he served eight-and-a-half years in prison before being released after Kenya won independence in 1963.

© DIAGRAM

party government led by Moi was widespread among the Kikuyu. Moi considered the Kikuyu threatening to his position, and in the 1980s he tried to remove Kikuyu members of his cabinet.

Language

The Kikuyu speak a language also called Kikuyu (or Gikuyu). It is one of the Bantu group of languages, which itself is part of the Benue-Congo language group. Many Kikuyu also speak Swahili (or Kiswahili), which is used as a common language in East Africa and is the national language of Kenya. Many Kikuyu also speak English, the country's official language.

Ways of life

Many Kikuyu have moved away from Kikuyuland to other parts of the country, where they work in a variety of jobs. The Kikuyu have a reputation for having a strong business sense, and many have succeeded as traders and importers and in running industries.

FARMING Those Kikuyu living in rural areas tend to practice farming. Before the arrival of the British, the Kikuyu farmed land until the soil was exhausted, and then moved to a fresh patch. Land was plentiful, and the Kikuyu had no need of crop rotation. Today, they have adopted different farming methods, with most making their living from continuous crop farming. The main crops grown include beans, corn, millet, potatoes, sugarcane, sweet potatoes, and a variety of vegetables. Colonialism introduced the Kikuyu to cash crops such as bananas, coffee, and *pyrethrum* – used for making insecticides. The Kikuyu also keep bees, goats, and sheep, and a few cattle.

Social structure

SOCIAL STRUCTURE Kikuyu society had a highly organized social structure originally based on nine *clans* (groups of extended families that share a common ancestor or ancestors); although only remnants remain of this social organization, the emphasis on the family is maintained. In addition, each person belongs to an *age-set*, called a *riika*. Which riika a person belongs to

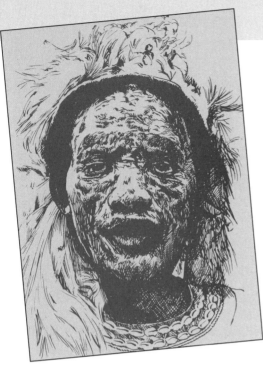

Ceremonial attire
This Kikuyu man is wearing ceremonial dress. Although modern Western-style clothes are more common nowadays, on special occasions and events some still wear more traditional outfits.

Ceremonial shields
Shields like these were used at initiation ceremonies for different periods in a male's *age-set*. They were used in dancing, but apparently not in warfare.

depends on the time they first undergo *circumcision*; this applies to both boys and – more controversially and with more serious, long-lasting consequences – girls.

POLITICAL STRUCTURE In the past, each village was ruled by a council of nine elders. These came from either one of the divisions found in each male age-set: *maina* or *mwangi*. The maina and mwangi subdivisions operate as the political leaders for alternate periods of between twenty and forty years. Every group of nine villages elected a representative to a higher council for an area known as *mbari*, or subclan. Each mbari sent a representative to a district council. The Kikuyu's system of landholding was based on the mbari. The councils acted as courts of law when necessary. The more senior elders served as high priests in the Kikuyu religion.

Culture and religion

RELIGION As a result of missionary activities in the earlier part of the 1900s, many Kikuyu are Christians and they have established their own, independent, churches. A minority still adhere to the Kikuyu religion, perhaps in conjunction with Christianity. The Kikuyu religion is founded on a belief in one all-powerful god called *Ngai*. According to legend, the Kikuyu are descended from one of Ngai's three sons, *Gikuyu*, who chose to be a farmer. Gikuyu married a wife provided by Ngai, named *Moombi*, known as the creator. She bore him nine daughters, each of whom had a family that became a clan, taking their mother's name. This, says tradition, is the origin of the nine main clans of the Kikuyu.

Beads for beauty
A beaded headdress was a popular form of decoration among Kikuyu women before most adopted Western-style clothing.

Mount Kenya
Mount Kenya, in the heart of the Kikuyu homeland, is 17,040 ft (5,198 m) high. It is thought to be the home of *Ngai*, god of the Kikuyu religion, and is called "Keré Nyaga," the "Mountain of Mystery" by the Kikuyu.

© DIAGRAM

Maasai

Giraffe-bone mortars
The pelvic bones of a giraffe have been used to make these mortars, used by *laibons* (healers and prophets) to grind medicine in. The Maasai have long been sculpting surrealistic artifacts based on the natural shapes of animals' bones. These mortars have been shaped to resemble elders' ears.

The Maasai are a collection of groups who live mostly in the grasslands of the Great Rift Valley that straddle the border of Kenya and Tanzania. The cattle-herding Maasai are often regarded as the Maasai "proper." Other Maasai groups include the Samburu of Kenya and the Arusha of Tanzania. There are over 250,000 Maasai.

History

The Maasai are Plains Nilotes (people originally from the southwestern fringe of the Ethiopian Highlands who migrated to the plains of East Africa). The ancestors of the Maasai initially settled to the east of the Great Rift Valley between mounts Kilimanjaro and Kenya. From the 1600s, the Maasai "proper" migrated southward while the Samburu turned east and settled in the mountains.

The 1700s were a period of increasing power and geographical expansion for the Maasai. Despite their relatively small numbers, by the early 1800s they dominated the region between Mount Elgon and Mount Kenya in the north and Dodoma, now the capital of

Maasai timeline

1600s	Maasai migrate southward from Rift Valley
1700–1800	Period of expansion and increasing power
1880s–1890s	Rinderpest (a cattle disease), cholera and smallpox epidemics spark famine
1885–1895	Britain and Germany partition East Africa
1904–1908	Maasai lands in British East Africa settled by Europeans
1961	Tanganyika wins independence
1963	Kenya wins independence
1964	Tanganyika and Zanzibar unite to form Tanzania
1965	Each part of Tanzania is allowed only one political party
1967	Arusha Declaration; Tanzania adopts socialism
1985	Tanzania abandons socialism
1991	Kenya allows for multiparty politics
1993	Maasai and Kikuyu clash in Kenya's Rift Valley
1995	Chaotic first multipartly elections held in Tanzania

Tanzania, in the south. As a rule they were not conquerors, but conflict with their neighbors or other Maasai groups began when they raided cattle or defended their own herds.

The nineteenth century was a period of increasingly frequent civil war among the Maasai. In particular, the Maasai "proper" – united for the first time under one leader, the *laibon* (prophet) Mbatiany – were in conflict with the Laikipiak, an agricultural Maasai group. This was followed by rinderpest (a cattle disease), smallpox, and cholera epidemics and famine during the 1880s and 1890s, which impoverished or killed thousands of Maasai. These disasters sparked further civil wars. This troubled period of Maasai history coincided with the British and German partition of East Africa. Maasai lands in British East Africa were taken over by European settlers and the Maasai were restricted to reserves.

Language

The Maasai speak a Nilotic language called Maa.

Ways of life

SEMINOMADIC PASTORALISM The majority of Maasai are *seminomadic pastoralists* (livestock raisers who move seasonally with their herds to make the best use of available water and pasture), herding mostly cattle and keeping a few sheep and goats. A minority, such as the Arusha, are farmers. Boys take the cattle out to graze by day and herd them back inside the village enclosure at night. Each family has its own cattle, but they are managed as part of a larger village herd. During the dry season, the Maasai men drive the cattle to distant water holes, making temporary camps until the rains come.

Maasai moran
Moran (the youngest *age-set*) sometimes wear their hair in thin braids. Painstakingly done by a friend, the braids are extended by interweaving them with string caked with *ocher* (a yellow or reddish-brown clay).

Battle dress
This line-up of *moran* shows them in full battledress. The feathered headdresses made it difficult for enemies to count their numbers. The Maasai frequently won their battles as they were well prepared both physically and psychologically. Their reputation for belligerence and ferocity, however, was largely fostered by Arab slave traders to scare competitors off inland trade routes.

© DIAGRAM

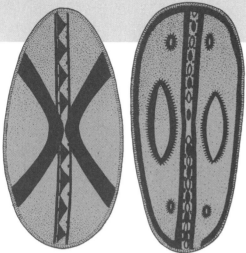

Shields
These Maasai shields are made from buffalo hide and weigh up to 50 lb (23 kg) each. They carry designs called *sirata* that indicate the *age-group* and family of the shield's owner. In battle, such shields would be carried with an 8 ft (2.5 m) long spear, but it is now illegal to carry a spear in Kenya.

The Maasai's pastoral way of life is under threat as their right to graze cattle over land historically dominated by the Maasai is being eroded. This process began under colonialism when white settlers were given Maasai lands to farm and group ranches were set up to bring the Maasai into the money economy – a process continued after independence under pressure from the World Bank. Under the independent Kenyan government, the Maasai ranches were divided into individual farms and a lot of land was sold to big landowners or allocated to well-connected non-Maasai people. In Tanzania during the socialist era of the 1970s and 1980s, a process called *villagization* placed dispersed populations such as the Maasai into settled villages. Fortunately, however, politicians are beginning to realize the efficiency of traditional herd management techniques and now try to combine them with new developments, for instance in veterinary care, instead of trying to eradicate them.

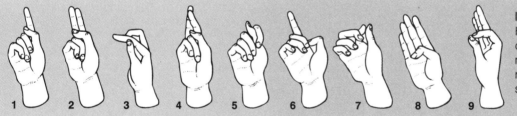

Numbering system
Hand signals are a common Maasai method of indicating numbers, and are still used today.

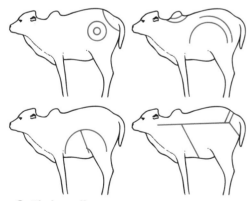

Cattle branding
Until recently, the Maasai would brand their herds. These marks identified the owners of the cattle. This practice has died out, however, as the Maasai now often sell the hides and can get a better price for unmarked ones.

Another threat to Maasai grazing lands has resulted from the loss of wildlife. Widely-roaming elephant and giraffe populations once helped maintain grasslands by grazing them, preventing the formation of dense *scrub* (or bush, dense vegetation of scraggly trees and shrubs). The boom in big-game hunting, which began during the colonial era and was succeeded by poaching, has allowed large tracts of grassland to convert to scrub, which cannot support cattle. One unique solution to this problem, adopted in particular by the Samburu, has been to change to camel herding. Camels are hardy animals that can feed from scrub; they can go for long periods without water; and the milk they produce is more nutritious, more plentiful, and lasts longer than cow's milk. They are also popular with tourists.

INDUSTRY Historically, few Maasai engaged in industry. Although some Maasai families have long been blacksmiths, they are despised by others and not allowed to intermarry. As their seminomadic lifestyle is curtailed, however, many Maasai have left the pastoral economy and sought employment in urban areas working in hotels and lodges or as security guards.

TOURISM The Maasai, who are sought out by visitors, have been greatly affected by tourism; some villages earn a considerable part of their income from sightseeing tours. These tourists expect the Maasai to appear "traditionally authentic," however, and this has to be balanced with the need to adapt to the changing economic climate. Much of the revenue earned through tourism does not reach the Maasai; a lot of the crafts marketed as Maasai are in fact neither manufactured nor sold by them. Some Samburu, however, organize camel safaris.

HOUSING During the dry season, Maasai men live in temporary camps. During the rainy season, they live in homesteads called *enkang*. These are usually built on high ground by women from cattle manure, mud, and grass. They are relatively permanent and are rebuilt every five to ten years. From time to time, the site of the village is moved. As the Maasai become more settled, however, enkang are increasingly being used as year-round homes. To cope with the greater demands on their homes, Maasai women have adopted new building techniques. Houses are often improved by adding a ferro-cement coating to the roof (a thin, watertight layer) and gutters to channel off rainwater into a container. Also, changes in the Maasai diet that have entailed more cooking have, in turn, led to the addition of chimneys.

DIET The Maasai diet was once based on milk, mixed with cattle blood at times of scarcity. Young men were supposed to stick strictly to a milk, blood, and meat diet; others could eat butter and honey. Only male elders could drink mead made from honey. If cows' milk was scarce, women could drink the milk of goats. Men were supposed to drink only cows' milk.

Maasai girl
This young Maasai girl is wearing beaded necklaces, earrings, and a beaded headband. Beadwork is a major art form in Africa and Maasai jewelry reflects this. Some Maasai girls do not consider themselves fully dressed without their jewelry.

© DIAGRAM

Wooden stick
A wooden stirring stick used in making butter from milk.

Calabash *(far left)*
This bottle is made from a long *calabash* (gourd). It has been decorated with leather and cowrie shells. Such bottles were once in common use among the Maasai. Now, they are more likely to be found in museums.

Maasai woman
Coiled-wire earrings, necklace, and armbands indicate that this woman is married and a mother.

The Maasai diet is now no longer restricted to milk, meat, and blood. In fact, milk with blood is rarely drunk today. Instead, the Maasai supplement their diet with tea, sugar, vegetables, and grains such as corn. Cattle, goats, and sheep are traded for these items.

CLOTHING Until recently, the Maasai usually wore clothes made from calfskin or buffalo hide. Women would wear long skirtlike robes and men shorter tunics. Greased with cow fat, such garments provided protection from both Sun and rain, were hard wearing, easily available, and did not need to be washed with water. As imported fabrics and Western clothes become the norm, however, greater pressure is put on limited water resources as these textiles need to be washed with water when soiled.

Social structure

AGE-GRADES Maasai society is organized into male *age-grades* (basically, the social hierarchy). Every man belongs to a particular *age-set* (a group of males who were initiated at the same time) and moves with this same set up through the various age-grades.

For their initiation into manhood, young men around the age of sixteen live in camps called *manyattas* away from the village. Here, they are taught about herd management, religion, politics, and the skills of social life. After they have undergone *circumcision* they join the youngest age-grade of *moran*, often translated as "warriors." Moran did act in the past as the Maasai army, but fighting is not their main function. The moran are usually responsible for the herds when they are far from the village during the dry season and provide a source of labor for specific tasks. Since the 1960s, many moran now complete their education after circumcision. The Maasai trace their history by referring to the time when particular age-sets were serving as moran.

After a period of between seven and fifteen years, all existing moran are upgraded to the status of elders. As elders they have the right to chew tobacco, take snuff, and settle, but at this stage they have little influence. The most recent age-set to become elders is called *ilterekeyani*.

74

There are two more grades of elder: senior and retired. Senior elders take decisions on such matters as disputes, allocation of pasture lands, and, in the modern world, development projects. Retired elders are still very influential and can act as patrons of men in younger age-sets.

COUNCILS Each age-set holds council meetings chaired by a nominee known as the *olaiguenani*. Every man can have his say and decisions are taken by consensus. If an issue affects other age-sets, then olaiguenani from the relevant groups meet. They cannot take decisions without referring back to their age-set though and they also consult with the women.

Culture and religion

RELIGION The Maasai worship one god, *Ngai*, the husband of the Moon. He is thought to dwell above Mount Kilimanjaro, Tanzania – Africa's highest mountain. Legend says that in the beginning Ngai created the Maasai and then created all cattle for them. In the past, this was used to justify raiding a neighbor's cattle. Now, disputes over cattle are more likely to be settled by negotiation than raiding.

The Maasai have great respect for their laibons, who are prophets, leaders of rituals, and healers. Their major function was once to advise the moran on advantageous times for raiding or war, and to bless their ceremonies. Laibons would also announce major prophecies from a trancelike state. In the present, laibons admit that their prophetic abilities are on the wane but they claim still to be able to divine the sources of personal misfortune; therefore, they now deal on an individual basis with clients who have problems such as infertility or bad luck rather than advise the whole community or foretell the future.

DANCING In a traditional Maasai dance, the performing moran would jump up and down, without using their arms, and grunt as they touched the ground. Moran would perform this dance in unison, keeping perfect time, and watched by other Maasai.

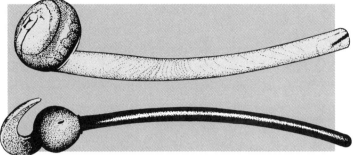

Orinkas

Orinkas are ceremonial clubs that men would carry to *age-group* meetings. In the past, age-group leaders carried ivory or rhinoceros horn orinkas, but the use of these materials is now illegal.

Bleeding cattle

Cattle are very important to the Maasai and are only killed on special occasions. Instead, their milk provides the staple food. At times of scarcity in particular, this milk would be mixed with blood from the cow to make it go further. The animal's jugular would be pierced, the blood caught, and then the wound would be stopped with mud or dung leaving the animal none the worse.

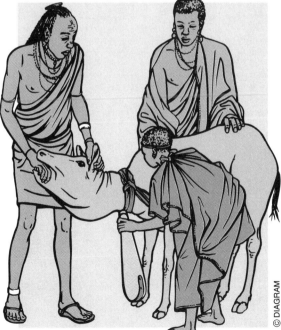

© DIAGRAM

75

How tourism affects the people of East Africa

Since the early 1970s, East Africa has been a major destination for tourists attracted to the region's varied landscapes, wildlife, and cultures. Tourism, however, is not new to East Africa; the region has been visited by European tourists since the late nineteenth century. Hunters — both tourists and white settlers — were responsible for what amounted to carnage, eliminating entire species such as the blaubok (a large, bluish-gray antelope) and quagga (a type of zebra). Hunters would take pride in slaughtering hundreds of animals on a single expedition: a safari led by former president of the United States Theodore Roosevelt slaughtered five thousand animals, including some of the few remaining white rhinos.

Tourism has become the single most important source of foreign currency and is central for development plans of most countries in the region. Some argue that tourism brings much-needed jobs to regions of high unemployment, but that ignores the fact that service jobs — in restaurants and hotels — are no replacement for the largely self-sufficient ways of life that many people have been able to maintain.

People, parks, and conservation

During the 1940s, in the name of conservation, huge tracts of land in East Africa were designated as parks, with admission reserved for rangers and paying tourists. These areas were not "wilderness," however, but were among the world's longest-inhabited areas: game being concentrated in regions that, with the best grazing land and most reliable water sources, were areas also most suitable for cattle and, of course, people.

Conflicts between the interests of indigenous peoples and wildlife conservation are well illustrated by the case of the Maasai. From the 1940s to the 1980s, Kenya's Maasai were deprived of most of their dry-season pasture because it was said that a human population could not coexist with wildlife within a park. Some conservationists have argued that local people have always endangered wildlife through hunting and overgrazing. Historically, peoples hunted only to survive, however, and most ecologists now agree that overgrazing was rare. Only after the Europeans arrived was wildlife threatened.

Trophy-hunters
Buffalo were among the many big-game animals of East Africa that were killed by European and American hunters seeking trophies. Unlike local people, who used every part of any animal caught and rarely killed more game than they needed, the trophy-hunters had no use for anything but the head or horns. In recent decades, while antihunting laws have protected the wildlife, conservation measures often adversely affect locals by keeping them out of the parks.

There is general agreement that environmental damage would result from unrestricted settlement in the parks. But many people argue that the Maasai at least be given grazing access. Instead, they are excluded from the best of the lands they regard as theirs, which leads to overgrazing elsewhere, with a result that many of the parks are islands of biodiversity set amid environmental degradation.

Not surprisingly, many of the Maasai expelled from parks feel bitter toward conservation and tourism. Some have taken to poaching, while others are actively hostile toward tourists.

Sea and sand
Coastal tourism in East Africa – particularly the main resorts of Mombasa and Malindi in Kenya – has been expanding without restrictions. Most Kenyan beach hotels have been built in tourist enclaves and have resulted in local people losing their land. Fishermen have lost access to beaches and fishing grounds because of hotel development and the

Hot-air ballooning
A hot-air balloon drifting over Masai Mara provides tourists with an aerial view of this national park, which straddles the border between Kenya and Tanzania. Hot-air ballooning is a popular tourist activity.

National parks and game reserves
The map above shows the major national parks and game reserves of Uganda, Kenya, and Tanzania. The establishment of these protected areas curtailed many people's rights of access to vital resources. Some were even evicted from their land. Today, governments are beginning to realize the value of indigenous lifestyles that help maintain the environment and are allowing greater access to national parks and game reserves.

(Names in brackets indicate peoples affected by the establishment of that park or reserve)

1 Ruwenzori
2 Lake Mburo (*Bahima*)
3 Kabelega Falls
4 Kidepo (*Dodoth, Ik, Napore, Nyangia*)
5 Siboli
6 Marsabit (*Boran*)
7 South Turkana (*Turkana*)
8 Mount Elgon (*Maasai*)
9 Laikipia (*Maasai, Laikipiak*)
10 Losai
11 Samburu (*Samburu*)
12 Buffalo Springs (*Samburu*)
13 Shaba
14 Aberdares (*Kikuyu*)
15 Mount Kenya
16 Meru
17 Masai Mara (*Maasai*)
18 Amboseli (*Maasai*)
19 Chyulu
20 Tsavo (West)
21 Tsavo (East) (*Taita*)
22 Shimba Hills
23 Serengeti (*Maasai*)
24 Ngorongoro Crater (*Maasai*)
25 Arusha (*Arusha*)
26 Tarangire
27 Mkomazi (*Maasai*)
28 Ruaha
29 Mikumi
30 Selous

© DIAGRAM

77

creation of marine parks, while local women can no longer collect crabs, once an important source of food. Scuba diving, reef trips, and sewage from hotels have damaged coral reefs, resulting in local resentment toward tourists.

Elsewhere in East Africa, coastal tourism is either in its infancy or tourist numbers are deliberately limited, so lessening both environmental damage and conflict with local people. This situation is likely to change with Tanzania – in particular on the island of Zanzibar – promoting its beaches.

Kilaguni
Tourists get the chance to see wildlife close-up at Kilaguni Lodge in Tsavo, Kenya's largest national park. Recently expanded to include a conference center, Kilaguni attracts a lot of tourist traffic.

Kenya

Tourism accounts for forty percent of Kenya's foreign currency earnings, with tourists drawn by the beaches and wildlife safaris. Because of the revenue from tourists, wildlife preservation has been important for the government. With a rising population, however, many Kenyans question the priority given to wildlife tourism, which excludes local people and limits the availability of much of the country's best land for agriculture. Furthermore, the costs of conservation are high and the upkeep of parks and reserves is dependent on foreign aid.

Uganda

Two decades of dictatorship and political unrest have meant that only since 1990 has Uganda been in a position to actively promote tourism. Uganda's rare mountain gorillas are its primary attraction, but water-based ecosystems are also promoted, including cruises to view crocodiles and hippos. In recent years, the creation of national parks has led to the displacement of entire peoples; in 1982, for example, the cattle-herding Bahima were expelled from their grazing land in what became Lake Mburo National Park.

Tanzania

Tourism contributes twenty-five percent of Tanzania's foreign currency earnings. As in Kenya, tourism is highly controversial due to the cost of conservation programs, population displacement, and a government legacy of

Treetops
In the Aberdares National Park, Kenya – once a Mau Mau stronghold – is Treetops Lodge, a world-famous hotel. It was first built in 1934 and has been visited by many European royals.

avoiding tourist development as being demeaning and culturally threatening. Foreign tour operators reap most of the financial benefits. This situation is gradually changing as the Tanzanian government encourages tourism away from the congested northern parks near the Kenyan border toward game reserves elsewhere and to Zanzibar's beaches. Nevertheless, the Maasai have been banned from the Ngorongoro Crater and Serengeti National Park – both of which, the country is proud to boast, have been declared

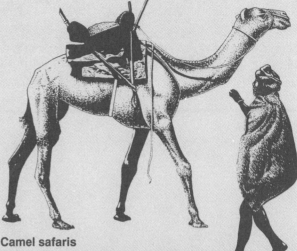

Photo opportunity
Here a tourist photographs a Maasai woman. People in traditional costume are popular with tourists and can earn welcome extra income by posing for photographs. Others, however, feel that this reinforces negative views of an unchanging, "primitve" Africa.

Camel safaris
Camels have been used in Somalia for centuries and, well suited to the environment, they have recently been introduced elsewhere in East Africa. This Samburu man leads a camel on a tourist trek in Kenya.

government is keen to limit the social and environmental damage that has blighted the East African mainland. The Seychelles is promoted as an upmarket destination, so bringing maximum revenue from as few tourists as possible. Half the land is designated as a park, but there is little conflict between tourists and islanders as most of the park area is unsuited to agriculture or human habitation.

World Heritage sites by the United Nations – forcing them into a more sedentary existence that does not suit their cattle-herding lifestyle.

Seychelles
Until the opening of the airport in 1971, only a handful of tourists visited the Indian Ocean islands of the Seychelles each year. Tourism is now the main foreign currency earner, but the Seychelles' Marxist

Local crafts
On a roadside in Kenya, this Kikuyu woman is selling bags and baskets, which are made from *sisal* and are called *ciondo*.

Nyamwezi

T he Nyamwezi live in west-central Tanzania where they are one of about 120 ethnic groups. There are between 1,000,000 and 1,500,000 Nyamwezi if not more. Their name, originally "Wanyamwezi" meaning "People of the Moon," was given because they came from the west, where the new Moon is first seen. Their homeland is known as Unyamwezi.

History

Oral history holds that the region of Unyamwezi was uninhabited until the seventeenth century. Then, chiefly families began to arrive from various directions. The earliest records are from the late 1600s, and concern the Galagansa, a western group. The Nyamwezi formed a number of semi-independent, self-governing units called *ntemi* (chiefdoms). A few powerful ntemi such as the Ha, Zinza, and Ngoni dominated the others.

By about 1800, traders from these groups were visiting the east coast – whose inhabitants gave them the name Wanyamwezi. The Nyamwezi gained a considerable reputation as pioneers of long-distance trade in East and

Nyamwezi timeline

1600s	Nyamwezi settle in present-day are of west-central Tanzania
1800s	Nyamwezi develop trade limks with east coast
1860–1870	Mirambo controls Ugowa and begins empire building
1871–1875	Mirambo frequently at war with Arabs from coast
1884	Death of Mirambo; empire begins to disintegrate
1885	German Protectorate includes Unyamwezi
1898	First "hut-tax" collected by Germans
1920	Britain administers Germany's East African colonies
1951	3,000 Africans evicted to make way for white farmers
1961	Tanganyika wins independence
1964	Tanganyika and Zanzibar unite to form Tanzania
1965	Each part of Tanzania is allowed only one political party
1967	Arusha Declaration; Tanzania adopts socialism
1985	Tanzania abandons socialism
1992	Tanzania introduces multiparty politics
1995	Chaotic first democratic elections held in Tanzania
1996	Thousands of refugees fleeing fighting in Burundi enter Tanzania. War crimes tribunal set up in Tanzania to deal with Rwandan and Burundi war criminals

Central Africa by organizing trading caravans. The principal trade was in iron – made and worked by the northern Nyamwezi – and salt. Later, copper and ivory, became the main commodities. There was also some slave trading. During the 1800s, the Nyamwezi bought guns and some groups established standing armies. There were several wars among the chiefdoms, and also armed conflict with the Arab traders from the coast.

In the nineteenth century, a ntemi chief named Mirambo managed to establish his dominance over several chiefdoms. Mirambo's short-lived empire came into conflict with Arab traders but broke up soon after his death in 1884. During the 1890s, German colonists took control of mainland Tanzania, which they ruled as German East Africa. Britain took over after World War I. In 1951, the British evicted 3,000 Africans from their land to make way for white farmers.

RECENT EVENTS Tanganyika became independent in 1961 and, on union with the island of Zanzibar in 1964, became Tanzania. In 1965, the two parts of Tanzania were allowed only one political party each and two years later the country adopted a policy of socialism and self-reliance set out under the Arusha Declaration. Attempts to reorganize Tanzanian society along socialist lines had limited success but great impact on all Tanzanians including the Nyamwezi. Agriculture, in particular, was widely affected by *villagization* policies – the creation of new rural villages (*ujamma*), collectives, and large farming cooperatives. Although the planned improvements in agricultural production were never realized, social benefits in the area of health and education were achieved. After the retirement, in 1985, of President Julius Nyerere – who oversaw the socialist era – the worsening economic crisis led to the abandonment of socialism. More pragmatic policies introduced since have helped the economy to recover.

Language
The Nyamwezi speak a language called Nyamezi (or Kinyamwezi). In addition, many Nyamwezi speak Swahili (or Kiswahili) and, or, English.

Gift figure
This wooden figure dates from the nineteenth century and was probably made by a Nyamwezi carver who accompanied an ivory-trading expedition to the island of Bukerebe in southeast Lake Victoria. It was presented by the traders to the Kerebe chief. The making and giving of such figures helped the traders enhance their standing with powerful chiefs.

Ntemi chiefs (below)
These two men were the chiefs of Kahima and Karitu chiefdoms in 1959. They are shown wearing their ceremonial robes, which are rarely seen today.

© DIAGRAM

Female figure (*left*)
The lack of feet on this carved, wooden figure suggests that it was formerly part of another piece, an altar perhaps. The figure is female and may have been used to represent the nurturing qualities of the person represented, probably a chief.

Staff (*right*)
This carved, wooden staff is 3ft (1m) long and would have been used as a status symbol by a *ntemi* (chief). It is simple and elegant in design and, like a lot of African art, both functional and aesthetic.

Houses
In the rural villages, traditional Nyamwezi houses are circular, with an internal cylinder that provides an interior room. The walls are trellislike structures, plastered from the inside with mud. This steep, conical roof is thatched. Today, some homes are rectangular and have metal sheeting on top.

Ways of life

AGRICULTURE Many Nyamwezi live and work outside their homeland where they are engaged in various professions. Nevertheless, for the majority, growing crops and raising animals is their livelihood. The territory of the Nyamwezi is undulating country, some of it forested or dry grassland, which is unsuitable for agriculture or grazing. There is a dry season lasting from May to October, and a wet season from November to April. Farming is mostly confined to the wet season. The Nyamwezi still cultivate some of their land with hand hoes, but plows drawn by oxen or tractors are becoming more common. Cereal crops include corn, millet, sorghum, and rice. Other food crops include beans, cassava, mushrooms, onions, *groundnuts* (peanuts), spinach, and tomatoes. Fruit crops include bananas and oranges. The major cash crops are cotton, sunflowers, rice, and tobacco. The Nyamwezi raise large numbers of cattle, and also keep, goats, sheep, and chickens.

TRADE Athough most people are dependent on agriculture, trading is still important. During the colonial era, Nyamwezi trading caravans to the coast ceased. Instead, the Nyamwezi were often engaged as porters. Many also came to be employed as migrant laborers and this is still true today. For many years, the independent Tanzanian government discouraged private trade as part of its socialist stance. More recently, private businesses have been encouraged and many Nyamwezi are now involved in trade again.

DIET The basic food is *bugalli*, a form of porridge made from grains and eaten with meat and vegetables. The Nyamwezi make beer from corn or sorghum, and also drink coffee and tea.

Social structure

Nyamwezi society is very open and well adapted to absorbing newcomers – including those from other ethnic groups. People who are not Nyamwezi but live among them are encouraged to follow their own ways of life and not to conform necessarily to Nyamwezi traditions. This cosmopolitan outlook on life could, in part, be thanks to their long history of trade and traveling for commercial reasons. As a result, many people regard themselves as Nyamwezi though their ancestors had no connection with any of the original groups. The political functions of the chiefs have now been abolished, but they still retain their social status.

Culture and religion

RELIGION A few Nyamwezi have converted to Christianity or Islam but neither of these religions have flourished among the Nyamwezi. Many still follow the Nyamwezi religion. Generally, the Nyamwezi believe in a supreme god, variously refered to as *Likube* (High God), *Limatunda* (the creator), *Limi* (the Sun), or *Liwelelo* (the Universe). This god is rarely worshipped directly. Ancestor reverence is the main component of the religion that is practiced daily. The ancestors of each family are thought to affect the lives of their descendants. Chiefs' ancestors, however, have a more widespread influence over all the inhabitants of their former domains. People make offerings, mostly of grain but occasionally of sheep or goats, to show respect to their ancestors, having first invoked the help of Likube.

There are also spirits who are believed to influence the lives of people and specific societies or cults are devoted to them. The *Baswezi* society, for example, recruits people who have been attacked or possessed by the *Swezi* spirit. Many people believe in *bulogi* (witchcraft) and attribute misfortunes or illness to its practice. Religious practitioners or *diviners* called *mfumu* are often consulted during trouble or illness; they interpret the belief system for their clients and use several methods to divine the forces active in a person's life and to arrive at remedies. Most mfumu act as medical consultants, using herbal medicines. The Nyamwezi are equally happy to make use of modern hospitals and medical facilities.

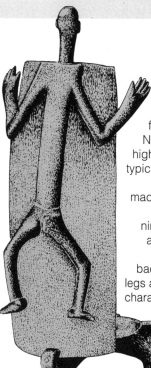

Chief's stool
One of the most famous pieces of Nyamwezi art, this high-backed stool is typical of those made for chiefs. It was made for the chief of Buruku in the nineteenth century and has a human figure on the backrest. The three legs are carved in the characteristic, curved Nyamwezi style.

Dancer (*below*)
Music and dancing are major Nyamwezi art forms. This man is wearing a traditional dancer's outfit. Long-familiar songs are sung at dances and weddings but new songs are always being composed.

© DIAGRAM

Nyoro

The Nyoro (or Banyoro) people live in the lakes region of northwestern Uganda. The main area they inhabit is bounded on its western side by Lake Albert and on the north and northeast by the Victoria Nile River and by the Muzizi River in the southeast. The southern borders are less clearly defined. There are over 250,000 Nyoro.

History

BUNYORO Nyoro history is centered around that of the medieval empire of Bunyoro-Kitara and later the Bunyoro Kingdom. Oral history attributes the founding of the first Bunyoro-Kitara Empire to the mythical Abatembuzi (or Tembuzi) people. They were succeeded by the Bachwezi (or Chwezi) dynasty (c. 1350 – c. 1500) about whom little is certain except that they were a immigrant, cattle-herding people. The Bachwezi established a centralized monarchy over the local Bantu peoples. They had a hierarchy of officials and also maintained an army. After the death of the last Bachwezi *bakama* (king), Wamara, the Bunyoro-Kitara Empire broke up into several separate states, one of which was Bunyoro. The Babito dynasty took control of Bunyoro

Nyoro timeline

1000s–1300s	Bantu–speakers migrate to lakes region of present-day northwest Uganda
c. 1350–c. 1500	Bachwezi dynasty rules over Bunyoro-Kitara Empire
c. 1500	Babito rule begins in Bunyoro
c. 1550	Bunyoro Kingdom at greatest extent
c. 1830	Babito prince founds independent Toro Kingdom
1859–1870	Bunyoro-Toro civil war
1870–1898	Reign of *Omukama* (King) Kabalega
1872	Battle of Baligota Isansa
1896	Bunyoro and Toro made British *protectorates* (colonies)
1900	Uganda Protectorate established; Bunyoro and Toro Kingdoms included
1962	Uganda wins independence; Milton Obote is Prime Minister
1966	Coup led by Milton Obote
1967	Bunyoro and Toro abolished
1971	Colonel Idi Amin Dada seizes power in military coup; he installs repressive regime
1979	Tanzanian forces and Ugandan rebels oust Amin
1980	Milton Obote elected President
1981–1986	Ugandan civil war; rebels led by Yoweri Museveni win power
1993	Buganda and Toro restored
1994	Nonparty elections held as first step to restoring democracy

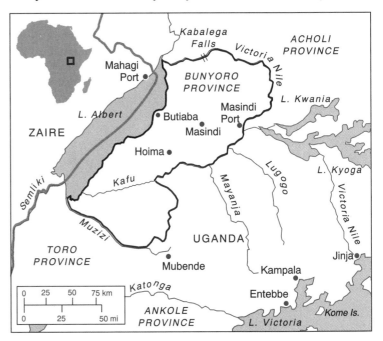

around the start of the sixteenth century. The Babito were originally Lwo-speaking River-Lake Nilotes – peoples who migrated from the Nile River in present-day southern Sudan to the lakes region of modern Uganda. Under their first *omukama* (ruler), Mpuga Rukidi, the Babito took over the country from the Bachwezi but kept many of the previous dynasty's rituals and customs. Raids against neighboring peoples expanded Bunyoro. By 1870, it extended to the north and east of the Nile and to the west of Lake Victoria.

Bunyoro was governed as a loose federation of *saza* (provinces) each under a chief appointed by the omukama. These saza were semi-independent and some on the edges of Bunyoro territory broke away to form independent states. During the long reign of Omukama Kyebambe Nyamutukura III (1786–1835), for instance, four of his sons turned against him. One of them, Kaboyo Omuhanwa, took the saza of Toro and established his own kingdom. Toro then became one of the border regions in dispute between the various Nyoro factions.

Omukama Kabalega (reigned 1870–98) tried to unite Bunyoro once again and regain the ascendancy it had lost on the rise of Buganda, a kingdom to the southeast. Kabalega created the *Abarusura*, a standing army of 20,000 men in ten divisions, each with its own commander. One division went to the capital Masindi to maintain law and order, under Kabalega's greatest general, Rwabudongo. Omukama Kabalega defeated the British in 1872 at the battle of Baligota Isansa, when they tried to set up an Egyptian *protectorate* (colony) in the northern part of Bunyoro. Kabalega later led a guerrilla war against the British for seven years until he was deported by them to the Seychelles in 1897. Toro and Bunyoro had already been made British protectorates in 1896. In 1900, they became part of the British Uganda Protectorate.

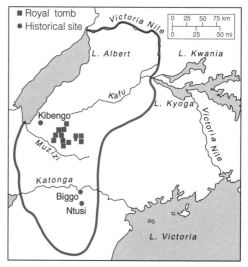

Bunyoro-Kitara Empire
This map shows the empire of Bunyoro-Kitara in the early sixteenth century, shortly before its disintegration. Bunyoro was the most important kingdom that emerged from its breakup. Although Bunyoro was influential and powerful, it never matched the Bunyoro-Kitara Empire in size.

Royal apperance
An *omukama* of Bunyoro is pictured outside his palace accompanied by his royal retinue.

© DIAGRAM

Milk pot

This pot, made from clay and burnished with graphite, was made at the beginning of the twentieth century. It would have been used to contain milk. Such pottery was reserved for the royal family and nobility. Normally, women would make pots, but royal pots are always made by men. The sling is made from fiber and allows the pot to be hung on a pole, usually in a line with others.

Omukama

This picture, taken in 1936, shows the (king) Bunyoro *omukama*, Sir Tito Winyi Gafabusa. Seated on the royal stool, he is wearing ceremonial robes and a crown reserved for certain court appearances. The Bunyoro Kingdom was abolished in 1967 but was restored in 1993. Sir Tito died before this in 1971.

RECENT EVENTS In 1962, Uganda gained its independence. In 1967, President Milton Obote abolished all of Uganda's kingdoms, including Bunyoro. From 1971 to 1979, Uganda was dictated to by its military ruler Colonel Idi Amin Dada. After he was ousted in 1979 by joint Tanzanian and Ugandan forces, the country was torn apart by civil war. After the end of this war in 1986, Uganda came under military rule until 1994. In 1993, Uganda's monarchies were restored but with ceremonial and cultural roles only. Solomon Gafabusa Iguru was crowned as Omukama of Bunyoro in 1994.

Language

The Nyoro speak a language also called Nyoro, which belongs to the Bantu group of languages.

Ways of life

AGRICULTURE Most Nyoro are farmers, living in scattered settlements, rather than villages. The most common cash crops are coffee, cotton, and tobacco. Bananas, usually beer-making varieties from which *mwenge* is brewed, are also used. The staple food is finger millet, although vegetables like sweet potatoes, cassava, peas, and beans are also grown. Corn cultivation is rapidly expanding both as a food and a cash crop. In precolonial times, the Nyoro were cattle farmers, but the herds were ravaged by the wars and rinderpest (a cattle disease) epidemics of the nineteenth century. Now the *tsetse fly* – which carries both cattle and human diseases – prevents large herds from being kept in modern Uganda. Instead, most farmers keep a few goats or sheep and chickens.

INDUSTRY Before Amin's era, Uganda had one of the richest economies in tropical Africa. Political insecurity, the expulsion of Ugandan Asians (who owned many businesses), hasty nationalization, and the civil war devastated Ugandan industries. This has affected the Nyoro as much as any other people in Uganda, despite improvements since the late 1980s, though locally based industries such as salt-making and blacksmithing have survived. Salt-making has been carried out by the Nyoro since the time of the Bunyoro Kingdom. Iron ore is plentiful and the Nyoro have long been skilled blacksmiths. In 1990, Uganda and Zaire agreed jointly to exploit petroleum reserves beneath Lake Albert. This will undoubtedly have an impact on the Nyoro, who live on the east of the lake.

Social organization

In the past, Nyoro people were divided into three main subgroups based on ethnic origin: the Babito (who took over Buganda from the Bachwezi), who always produced the hereditary omukama; the aristocratic, cattle-owning Bahima *pastoralists* (livestock raisers); and the Bairu cultivators, the largest group. While the Bairu are indigenous to the region, the Babito and the Bahima originally arrived as invaders. Intermarriage and mixing over the years, however, has blurred any ethnic basis for distinction between the three groups. Today, the divisions are more a matter of class than ethnicity or occupation – if they are considered at all. The Babito were originally Lwo-speaking peoples while the Bairu spoke a Bantu language. All Nyoro now speak the same language.

Culture and religion

RELIGION The Nyoro are predominantly Christian, though a few are Muslims. Many Nyoro still follow the Nyoro religion, inherited from the Bachwezi Empire in which the rulers were viewed as hero-gods. Even after the Bachwezi dynasty ended, senior mediums of the Bachwezi gods passed on advice to the omukama on how to maintain his personal fertility, achieve success in warfare, and promote the fruitfulness of the land. As well as being thought of as the ancient rulers of the kingdom, the Bachwezi gods are each associated with a place, event, element, or idea. For example, *Mugizi,* is the god of Lake Albert; *Nduala,* the god of pestilence; *Muhingo,* the god of war; and *Kaikara* the harvest goddess.

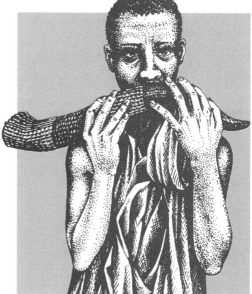

Trumpeter
The Nyoro leader's retinue always included special trumpeters, who performed at biennial festivals held to celebrate and renew the kingship. The trumpets are made from a gourd, covered with hide, and decorated with cowrie shells.

Bachwezi defenses
The Bachwezi dynasty constructed large earthworks for defensive reasons. This example at Biggo in Bwera district, Uganda, lies on a tributary of the River Katonga and must have had a role in defending the southern border of Bunyoro-Kitara. It is a system of trenches and ditches that extends over 6.5 miles (10.5 km) and would have protected large herds of cattle. It also has a royal enclosure, or *orirembo*.

© DIAGRAM

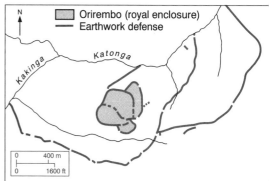

Orirembo (royal enclosure)
Earthwork defense

87

Oromo

The Oromo are a large ethnic group living in Ethiopia. Other African peoples call them Galla, a name the Oromo themselves dislike. Their territory, Oromia, covers southeastern Ethiopia and part of northern Kenya. It is almost as large as Texas in the United States and was once an independent country.

Estimates of the total number of Oromo vary between 2,500,000 and 25,000,000. They probably make up roughly half of the population of Ethiopia. There are nine main subgroups. They are the Arusi, Bararetta, Borana, Itu, Macha, Randili, Tulama, Walega, and Wollo. Altogether, there are about 200 different subgroups.

History

The Oromo are a Cushitic people. The Cushites originated in the Ethiopian Highlands and were the first food producers in East Africa. Historians think that the ancestors of the Oromo lived in Ethiopia at least 5,000 years ago. From the highlands of Ethiopia the Cushites gradually expanded to occupy most of northeast Africa, slowly migrating south and east to their present homeland. They began expanding northward in the

Oromo timeline

1500s	"Great Migration" into highlands of Ethiopia
1600s– **1700s**	Oromo begin to expand southward and settle
1788	Begemder Kingdom founded
1825– **1850**	Sudanese slave trade flourishing in Oromia
1850s– **1890s**	Oromo monarchies in southwest Ethiopia
1853	Begemder king overthrown
1889– **1896**	Oromo influence in decline in East Africa
1935– **1941**	Ethiopia invaded and occupied by Italy
1961	Ethiopian civil war begins
1974	Military coup overthrows Haile Selassie I; Ethiopia declared a socialist state
1975	Oromo Liberation Front (OLF) formed; active near Kenyan and Sudanese borders
1977	Maj. Mengistu Haile Mariam takes power in Ethiopia
1980s	Severe *droughts* cause famine throughout decade. OLF support increases
1991	Mengistu loses power; OLF part of new government; end of civil war and Eritrean liberation from Ethiopia follows
1992	OLF leaves government after dispute; renews rebellion; 20,000 Oromo detained
1994	Ethiopia organized into nine states based on ethnicity; Oromo state formed
1995	Small OLF bands still active. Dr Negasso Gidado elected Ethiopian president. 280 Oromo rebels on trial. Persecution of Oromo peoples continues

1500s, and by 1563 they controlled about one-third of Ethiopia. Sometime after 1600 they began raiding southward, and by 1699 they had reached Malindi, Kenya. In 1788 one of their chiefs, Ali, founded the Kingdom of Begemder in central and northwest Ethiopia. Other Oromo chiefs founded kingdoms in the early 1800s. Oromo chiefs served as ministers in the Ethiopian government, which they dominated.

In 1853 Kassa, a former bandit, overthrew Ras Ali of Begemder and married the successor to the Begemder throne. In 1855, he made himself emperor of Ethiopia, with the title of Tewodros (or Theodore) II. Later he was overthrown by a British expeditionary force. In 1880, Menelik II, the Amhara ruler of the Ethiopian province of Shoa, began to overrun Oromia. He became emperor of Ethiopia in 1889, and by 1900 had completely conquered Oromia. Menelik made the Oromo into slaves, and he and Queen Taitu personally owned 70,000 of them. The unfortunate Oromo fared little better under the last Ethiopian emperor, Haile Selassie I (reigned 1930–74), or under the Italians, who occupied the country from 1935 to 1941. Thousands of Oromo died in the civil war that racked Ethiopia from the 1960s to 1991. In this war, the Oromo and other ethnic groups strove to win independence. By 1993, only the Eritreans had attained it. Since 1995, the Oromo have been increasingly victimized with Oromia virtually under army occupation and many Oromo have become victims of summary rape, torture, or execution at the hands of government troops.

Language
The Oromo language is also called Oromo, and is one of the Cushitic language group.

Ways of life
The Oromo were originally a cattle-herding people, moving from place to place. Many, particularly in the lowlands of the south, are still *pastoralists*. They keep cattle, sheep, and goats, with donkeys as beasts of burden.

Market day
An Oromo woman, wearing a colorful headscarf, sells coffee beans at an open-air market. Her silver jewelry incorporates Austrian Maria Theresa dollars. These were once used as a trading currency in Ethiopia.

© DIAGRAM

Some groups have horses and camels, and one small group keeps pigs. They do no hunting or fishing, and milk, meat, and butter are the main items of their diet. In the highlands they are sedentary farmers, growing cereals and coffee as well as keeping animals, including chickens and goats.

DIVISION OF LABOUR Work is divided between the sexes: men tend to do all the herding, while women do the milking and look after the plants. The Oromo cultivate the soil with plows, drawn by pairs of oxen.

CLOTHING Clothing varies from one subgroup to another. In isolated areas traditional dress predominates. This includes, for men, a *waya*, a togalike garment, or a short kilt, and, for women, leather skirts, often with a cotton top. Men generally wear their hair short, while women have many elaborate hairstyles.

Social structure

In their days of independence, the Oromo were governed under a democratic system called the *gadaa*. The leaders were elected by adult males who had attained certain grades in the gadaa system. There were eleven of these grades, the first three being for boys. The sixth grade, also called gadaa, was that of the ruling class. Its members held office for only eight years. After that they became advisers for three grades, totaling twenty-four years. At the final grade they were retired. The system provided training so that when men entered the gadaa grade they were fully equipped to run their local government. The gadaa system has been in existence for more than five centuries. Under the republican government of Ethiopia, the system has declined and many of its attributes are banned, though in principle it still exists.

Goatskin containers
This Oromo woman is filling a container called a *gerber* with water. Gerbers are made from whole goatskins; the leg, tail, and neck openings have been tied shut.

Traditional architecture
Different types of house are generally associated with different Oromo subgroups.
1 Beco house
2 Shoa house
3 Arusi house
Elaboration includes adding verandas, providing a shady, porchlike area. Inside, they are divided into several compartments.

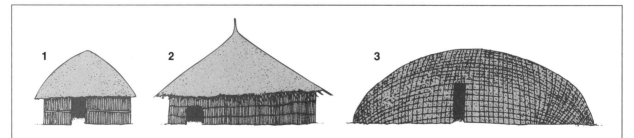

Culture and religion

The Oromo have a rich culture, which is slowly being eroded by their position within Ethiopia. They had their own calendar, based on a lunar month of twenty-nine days. The Oromian year is 354 days long, so their calendar is out of step with the Sun. Each day of the month has its own name, but as there are only twenty-seven names, each month begins on a different day. In many parts of Oromia, the Oromo calendar has given way to the Muslim calendar.

RELIGION Most Oromo follow either Islam or Christianity, and some still practice the Oromo religion, which features one supreme god, *Waqaayo*, plus a great many *ayanas*, or saints. Religious leaders are known as *quallus*, and their office is hereditary. There are also female religious leaders, *qalittis*. Some Muslim and Christian Oromo follow the Oromo religion at the same time. Islamicization was made easier by the Oromo's eagerness to resist the domination of the Amhara, who are predominantly Christian.

The Oromo believe in life after death. They used to hold a special prayer ceremony before the annual harvest, but the republican government of Ethiopia has made the ceremony illegal. The Oromo religion and its practices have survived mainly in southern Ethiopia. These practices include ceremonies to honor or celebrate birth, *circumcision*, marriage, and death.

ARTS AND CRAFTS Oromo blacksmiths make tools, spears, and other objects from iron. Goldsmiths make ornamental work such as bracelets from gold, which is panned in Oromia, and from silver. The silver is imported, mainly in the form of Maria Theresa dollars. These old Austrian coins were used as currency in East Africa for many years, and were still being minted in the twentieth century – always dated 1780. Oromo woodworkers fashion tools and plows, spears and bows, and simple tables. They make small barrels that are hung in trees as beehives. Some honey barrels are made of reeds. Weavers make plain cloth on simple looms.

Oromo granary
This *granary* (storehouse for grain) is made from woven sticks and has a conical thatched roof. Oromo houses and other buildings vary from one subgroup to another.

Holy tomb
The Oromo make frequent pilgrimages to the shrines or tombs of saints and holy figures. This is the tomb of an ancient miracle-worker called Sheikh Hussein and it is visited by people hoping to benefit from its healing powers. The tomb has been covered with colorful cloths to mark a celebration.

© DIAGRAM

East African hairstyles: the practical and the fantastic

In East Africa the men generally wear more elaborate hairstyles than the women do, many of whom shave their heads. Young Maasai men, for instance, might spend hours doing one another's hair. Many of the elaborate styles worn by Oromo men are said to resemble the highly stylized coiffures seen in Ancient Egyptian art.

Aside from shaving, one of the most common women's styles is the shiruba, which is composed of many tiny braids that are worn close to the scalp and loose at the ends, fluffing out at the back and over the shoulders. The style, which can take several hours to create, would normally be worn for up to week before being redone. "Western"-style hairdos are also being increasingly adopted, especially by urban women.

Although hairstyling all over the world is a means of personal adornment, it could be said that practicality dictates many of the styles worn in East Africa today, even some of the elaborate ones. Shaving all or most of the hair, cropping bangs over the forehead, and wearing tiny braids secured to the head are all ways of controlling hair that may take time to achieve but which give a conveniently long-lasting style. In contrast, hairstyles described by some nineteenth-century European travelers in East Africa were fantastic productions involving, for example, huge spikes or hoops — so fantastic, in fact, that they might well have been products of European imagination or exaggeration.

Pins and haircombs are among the accessories commonly used by East African women in their hair. They may be made of ivory, wood, and even silver (among Amhara women living in the Ethiopian Highlands especially). Other materials used in hairstyling include feathers, beads, rings,

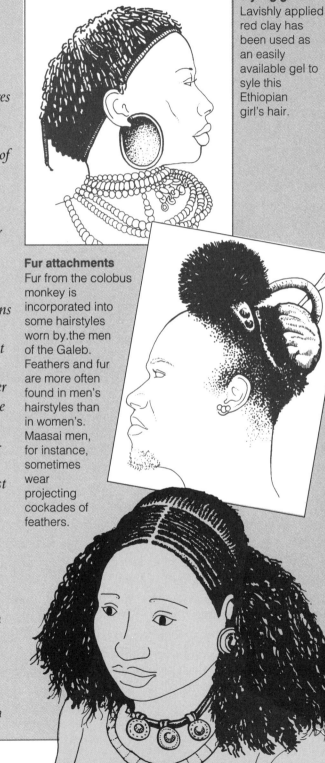

Styling gel
Lavishly applied red clay has been used as an easily available gel to syle this Ethiopian girl's hair.

Fur attachments
Fur from the colobus monkey is incorporated into some hairstyles worn by.the men of the Galeb. Feathers and fur are more often found in men's hairstyles than in women's. Maasai men, for instance, sometimes wear projecting cockades of feathers.

Shiruba style (right)
This Tigre girl from Ethiopia is sporting a typical shiruba hairstyle – braided at the top and loose at the ends.

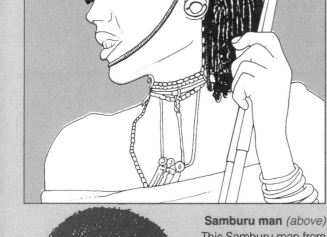

and grass; in southwestern Ethiopia, some women wear tiaras made of woven grass. Beads or pieces of bamboo might be used to close the ends of braids.

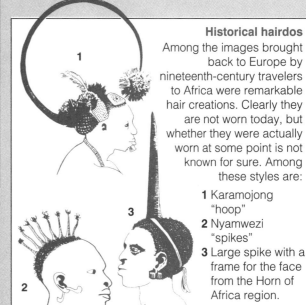

Historical hairdos

Among the images brought back to Europe by nineteenth-century travelers to Africa were remarkable hair creations. Clearly they are not worn today, but whether they were actually worn at some point is not known for sure. Among these styles are:

1 Karamojong "hoop"
2 Nyamwezi "spikes"
3 Large spike with a frame for the face from the Horn of Africa region.

Samburu man *(above)*

This Samburu man from Kenya wears a hairstyle that protects his eyes from the glare of the Sun. It has been created using *sisal*, cloth, *ocher*, and animal fat.

Boran woman *(left)*

This woman from Borana in the south of Ethiopia has elaborately braided hair. Near the roots, the braids are close to the scalp but are then left to hang free.

Maasai warriors

Traditionally, the Maasai people spend a lot of time on personal adornment and beauty, and this is particularly true of the younger adult men, or *moran*. They shave their heads when they first become moran, and later grow their hair long. A moran might have a friend spend a day or longer creating an elaborate style. A typical style for a moran incorporates hundreds of twisted strands of hair that have been smeared with clay and *ocher*, a reddish clay. Strands at the front would be brought together over the forehead. Maasai women, on the other hand, often adopt a more practical and infintely simpler style, first shaving and then smearing their heads with fat and ocher.

Somalis

T here are over seven million Somalis, most of whom live in Somalia, where they make up approximately seventy-five percent of the population. In addition, two million Somalis live in eastern Ethiopia, 100,000 in Djibouti, and 240,000 in northeast Kenya. Political turbulence in the 1980s and 1990s has caused thousands of Somalis to seek refuge in neighboring countries as well as outside Africa, especially in Yemen, Saudi Arabia, Italy, and Britain.

History

The Somalis' origins are uncertain, but by 1000 what is now Somalia was home to Cushitic people who had migrated from the Ethiopian Highlands. These people developed close contacts with Arabs and Persians who had settled on the coast. Through marriage and cultural and commercial ties the Somali people gradually emerged from these different groups. Between the eleventh and thirteenth centuries, the Somalis converted to Islam. During this period, their influential *clans* (several extended families who claim descent from a common

Somali timeline

900s	Arab trading post at Mogadishu
900s–1500s	Somalis disperse around present area of occupation and convert to Islam
1500s–1800s	Somali migrants settle in Ogaden region of Ethiopia
1884–1886	Italians, British, and French divide Somali lands
1900s–1920s	Somalis revolt against British, Ethiopian, and Italian colonists
1960	Somalia wins independence
1963	Ethiopian Somalis begin revolt
1964	Somalia at war with Ethiopia
1969	Muhammad Siad Barre leads military coup in Somalia
1974	Military coup overthrows Haile Selassie in Ethiopia
1975–1980s	Somalia organizes and funds Somali rebel groups in Ethiopia
1977	Djibouti wins independence. Maj. Mengistu Haile Mariam takes power in Ethiopia.
1980s	Drought and famine in Ethiopia
1981	Rebel Somali National Movement (SNM) formed in Somalia
1988–1992	Civil war and *drought* cause severe famine in Somalia
1989	Kenyan Somalis victimized
1991	Mengistu loses power in Ethiopia. Civil war begins after Barre ousted in Somalia; northern Somalia declares "independence"
1992–1995	US-led United Nations forces deployed to ensure the distribution of humantarian aid in Somalia
1995	Gen. Muhammed Farrah Aideed declares himself "president" of Somalia
1996	Aideed is killed; his son, Hussein Muhammad Aideed succeeds

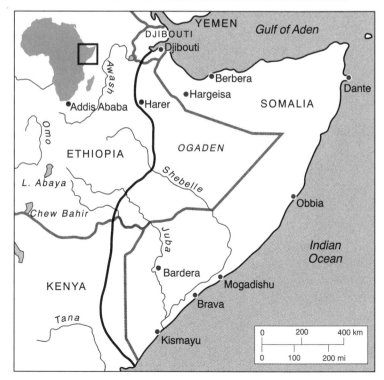

ancestor or ancestors) originated – the founding fathers of which, according to tradition, were related to the Prophet Muhammad and came from Arabia. By 1500, Somalis were raiding eastern Ethiopia (where they pushed the Oromo people out of the Ogaden region) and were expanding their territory southward. The Somalis gradually consolidated their position, but in the late nineteenth century, Britain, France, Italy, and Ethiopia divided Somali territory into separate colonies.

RECENT EVENTS In 1960, British (northern) and Italian (southern) Somaliland united to form the independent state of Somalia. After independence, rivalry between northern and southern Somalia mounted, and the government was accused of corruption. In 1969 the army, led by Major General Muhammad Siad Barre, staged a coup and abolished the elected parliament. For the next two decades, Somalia was under Barre's personal control.

Due to Somalia's strategic importance, Barre obtained foreign economic and military support, first from the former Soviet Union (USSR) and later from the United States (US). The weapons that these superpowers poured into the region enabled Somalia and Ethiopia to enter into disastrous wars with each other in 1964 and again in 1977, helped create a "gun culture" in the country, and provided Barre with the means to brutally persecute rival clans.

In the late 1980s, there emerged organized opposition to Barre and, with the end of the Cold War, the US ceased to support him. In January 1991, Mogadishu fell to rebel forces and, in May, the northern area declared independence as the "Somaliland Republic." Somalia's civil and political institutions collapsed, with opposition leaders unable to exert control. Into this power vacuum stepped armed factions, loosely allied to a clan or subclan. The breakdown of Somalia led to widespread famine and, with food deliveries from abroad interrupted by armed gangs, the United Nations attempted unsuccessfully to impose order between 1992 and 1995. By 1996, a fragile peace had returned to Somalia, but the country still remains divided today.

Camels
Camels are vital in the Somalis' semidesert environment as they can survive for long periods without water. Camels have long been used to transport both possessions and goods. The camels are Arabian dromedaries (single-humped).

© DIAGRAM

Education
Schooling among rural Somalis tends to be for boys. This student is studying Arabic at an Islamic school that teaches about the Arabic language and Islam.

Off to market
A Somali woman going to market. Women carry their wares on their heads, with more bulky items on the backs of donkeys. This lady is carrying a marrow.

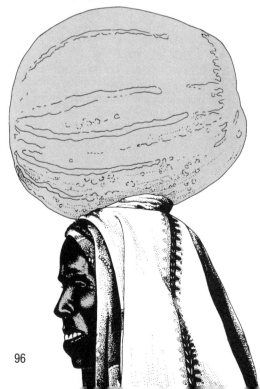

Backed by the Somali government, Ethiopian Somalis have been agitating for union with Somalia for many years. Rebel groups were particularly active from the 1960s until the mid-1980s. Ethiopia's new constitution, introduced in 1994, however, established a separate Somali state within the republic. This has helped to ease the situation somewhat. Kenyan Somalis have often found themselves used as political pawns between the Kenyan and Somali governments. The situation briefly improved after Barre renounced his claim to northeastern Kenya in 1981. In 1989, however, the Kenyans accused Somalis of poaching elephants, and many thousands were evicted from around game parks while others had their Kenyan nationality questioned.

Language
The Somali language is also called Somali. Somali has been heavily influenced by Arabic, but has been written in the Roman script since 1972.

Ways of life
Somalia's contrasting climate and terrain have led to the development of many different ways of life. The north and centre is mostly semidesert and dry grassland, with little rainfall and without permanent rivers. Here crops are grown only in the highlands, with wells providing a year-round water supply. The south is largely low-lying and fertile, and is watered by the Juba and Shebelle rivers.
NOMADIC PASTORALISM Most Somalis are *nomadic pastoralists*, who herd goats, sheep, cattle, and camels, with herd management based on migrating between water holes and pastures. Camels, which provide milk and meat as well as serving as a means of transportation, are especially suited to dry areas since they can survive for many days without water.

Nomad encampments are typically occupied by between five and ten families (that generally consist of a man, his wives and children, and elderly or unmarried relatives) who live in tents or temporary houses, which are surrounded by a stockade, made of thorn branches, where goats and sheep are kept at night. These animals are tended by women and children. Camels, kept outside the stockade area, are herded and milked only by men.

FARMING In the south, between the Shebelle and Juba rivers, are farmers who grow bananas, citrus fruits, corn, cotton, millet, sorghum, and sugar cane. Historically, nomadic Somalis regarded these people as inferior and not true Somalis. In recent years, many have had their land confiscated by more powerful, armed groups.

Social structure

CLANS The Somalis are divided into six major clans or *qabiil*: the Daarood, Hawiye, Issaq, Dir, Digil, and the Rahanwayn. In turn, these are divided into numerous subclans. Northern Somalia is dominated by the Samaale group, which comprises the Daarood, Dir, Hawiye, and the Issaq clans. They are mostly pastoral nomads. The Sab group, consisting of the Digil and Rahanwayn clans, dominates the south, and its members are generally farmers. Organization into clans has enabled the region's scarce resources to be shared peaceably, with disputes over water and pastures mediated by clan leaders. At times, however, the clan system can be extremely fragile as allegiances between subclans often shift.

MARRIAGE It is customary for marriages to be contracted between men and women of different clans, thereby extending clan alliances. Although women are able to count on the protection of both their parents' and their husbands' clans, during times of conflict they have had to choose between allegiance to one clan or the other. Nevertheless, even at the height of the civil war, this dual position has enabled women to serve as important channels of communication between warring clans, since their status has permitted them to travel between clans.

Culture and religion

RELIGION The vast majority of Somalis are Muslims.

POETRY There is a long tradition of Somali epic poetry, which has always been transmitted orally. Poems are frequently complex and draw upon history, a poet's personal experience, politics, or debate. Poets recite or chant their poems at both formal and informal occasions.

Milk pot
A Somali artisan made this wooden pot for holding milk. The surface has been stained black and then a decorative pattern has been carved, revealing the light wood beneath.

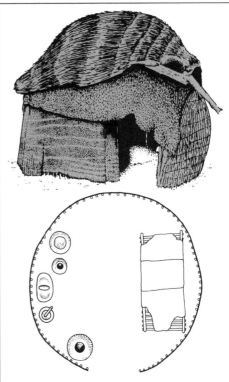

A typical home
Pastoral nomads live in tents made of brushwood and reeds that can easily be dismantled and transported. Also shown is a plan of the interior, which contains a bed and various jars and cooking tools.

© DIAGRAM

Swahili

The Swahili people live in the coastal regions and on the small offshore islands of Kenya and Tanzania. Their name is derived from an Arabic word and means "coast dwellers." There are between 200,000 and 400,000 Swahili people.

History

The Swahili people are of mixed Black African, Arab, and Persian descent. The coastal Black Africans were mainly Bantu and Cushitic groups who had migrated into the area from the northwest, and some Bantu from the south, before 1000. After the Bantu people, came the Arabs and Persians from southwest Asia. Most were attracted by the trade in ivory, skins, and slaves, though some were seeking refuge from political or religious persecution. By the start of the first millennium, there were Arab settlements in Mogadishu, Lamu, Malindi, Zanzibar, and Kilwa. Some of the settlements were ruled by Arabs and others by Africans. Around 1200, Persians from Shiraz established the Shirazi dynasty on the Banadir coast around Mogadishu.

Swahili timeline	
1000 BCE –	
1000 CE	Bantu and Cushitic peoples migrate into East Africa
900s	Arab trading posts established at Mogadishu and Kilwa
by 1100s	A distinct Swahili culture exists
c. 1150	Mombasa and Malindi founded
c. 1200	Persian Shirazi dynasty founded near Mogadishu
1200s	Mogadishu the preeminent port
c. 1400	Kilwa most important trading center on east coast
c. 1270	Kilwa starts minting coins
c. 1470	Mombasa begins period of growth; Kilwa declines
1498	Vasco da Gama in East Africa
1502–1509	Portuguese conquer East African coast to control trade
1699	Omani Arab traders control much of coast
1822–1837	East African coast under rule of the sultan of Oman
1832	Zanzibar made Omani capital
1840–1880s	Height of Swahili/Arab slave trade in East Africa
by 1900	Most Swahili under either German or British rule
1961–1963	Kenya, Tanganyika, and Zanzibar win independence
1964	Tanganyika and Zanzibar unite to form Tanzania
1965	Each part of Tanzania is allowed only one political party
1967	Arusha Declaration: Tanzania adopts socialism
1985	Tanzania abandons socialism
1991	Kenya allows multiparty politics
1993	Tension between Muslims and Christians in Tanzania
1995	Chaotic first multiparty elections held in Tanzania

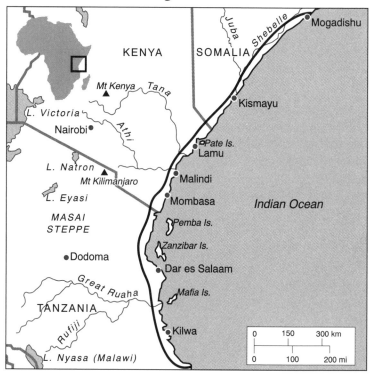

Printed khanga cloth
A *khanga* cloth is a large rectangle of cotton, printed with a border and a central design that usually incorporates a Swahili proverb. These were originally block-printed by hand – a technique introduced by the Omani Arabs. In recent times, khanga cloths are more likely to have been mass produced at a modern textile factory.

GOLDEN AGE Swahili culture emerged from the intermingling – mainly through marriage and trade – of these Arab, African, and Persian groups. By the 1100s at the latest, the Swahilis had emerged as a distinct people. They had a number of small kingdoms based on trading cities up and down the coast. One of the most important was Kilwa. Here, gold, gum, ivory, slaves, and lumber from inland were traded for cotton, glass, porcelain, and pottery, supplied by Arabian, Chinese, and Indian merchants. Kilwa was just one of about forty such ports along the East African coast, and on the islands of Pemba and Zanzibar, which are now part of Tanzania. The ruins of their stone buildings and palaces still survive.

FOREIGN DOMINATION This golden age of Swahili culture came to an abrupt end when Portuguese adventurers arrived on the coast, at first in 1498. By 1509, the Swahili had lost their independence to the Portuguese. In the seventeenth century, Omani Arab traders began to settle on the East African coast, driving out the Portuguese. They controlled most of the region by 1699 and between 1822 and 1837 the coast was ruled over as part of the Omani Empire. During this period, the Omani sultan, Seyyid Said, transferred his capital from Muscat in Oman to the island of Zanzibar, in order to gain control of the trade routes. Zanzibar dominated East African trade and became an international trading depot during the

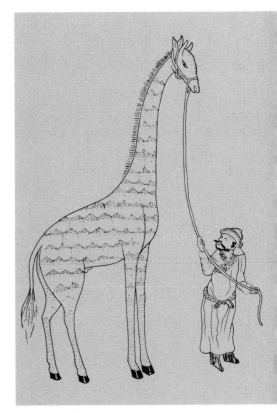

A gift to a Chinese emperor
This Chinese painting on silk shows the giraffe sent by the Swahili ruler of Malindi to the Ming Emperor of China, Ch'eng Tsu, in 1414. The emperor received a second giraffe from Malindi three years later.

© DIAGRAM

99

nineteenth century. Of particular importance in its prosperity was the slave trade. This was stimulated by the development of Arab plantations of cloves and coconuts on the East African coast and its islands, and French sugar plantations on islands in the Indian Ocean. Caravans began to be sent to the interior of East Africa as far south as present-day Malawi to collect slaves and many Arab and Swahili traders made their fortunes in this destructive trade. By the 1860s, 70,000 people a year were being sold as slaves at the Zanzibar slave market. Zanzibar declined with the abolition of the slave trade and the advent of German and British colonists.

RECENT EVENTS By 1900, Britain and Germany had taken control of Zanzibar and the mainland regions covered by the modern states of Kenya and Tanzania. Kenya, Tanganyika, and Zanzibar became independent in the early 1960s. In 1964, Tanganyika and Zanzibar united to form Tanzania.

Language

The Swahili language is called Swahili (or Kiswahili), and it belongs to the Bantu group of languages. Swahili contains about 20,000 Arabic words and has borrowed others from English, Persian, Portuguese, Urdu, and Gujarati. Swahili is not confined to the Swahili and it is widely spoken by many other people – about 30,000,000 altogether. Swahili is the official language of Tanzania

Carved doors
This carved door was made by a Swahili craftsman around the beginning of the twentieth century. Its structure – two panels that open inward from the central bar – is typical. The quality and size of such external doors served as an indicator of the household's wealth and status. The carving of doors reached a zenith in the eighteenth century when it was boosted by the wealth of Zanzibar. The carving on this door is relatively simple compared to that on some of the doors that belonged to the Zanzibari elite.

An ancient board game
Mankala is a game that has been played for at least 7,000 years and versions of it can be found throughout Africa as well as the rest of the world. This board was made by a Swahili craftsman in Tanzania. The object of the game is to capture the opponent's seeds. Players move seeds around a board, which is carved with a series of cups. It is a highly skilled game requiring a keen mathematical mind.

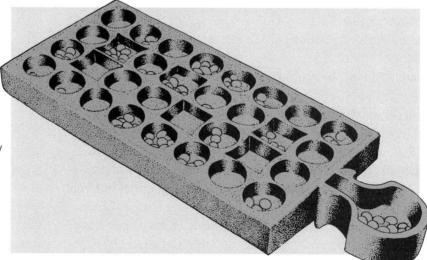

and one of the national languages of Kenya and Uganda, it is spoken by some people in Djibouti, Somalia, Mozambique, and Madagascar, and a dialect is the main language in the Comoros Islands, which lie in the Indian Ocean between Madagascar and Mozambique. Those people (about 1,000,000) who have Swahili as their mother tongue are called Waswahili, but they are not necessarily ethnic Swahili. Pidginized versions of Swahili are spoken in some parts of East Africa. A pidgin language is a grammatically simple one that combines elements of one or more languages. Pidgin Swahili is used as a common language by people of different nationalities, particularly in trade. An attempt was begun in 1925 to standardize Swahili. The Germans, who ruled what is now Tanzania, helped to spread the Swahili language by using it in their administration.

Ways of Life

The Swahili live in mixed societies alongside other ethnic groups. The coastal area where they mostly live is a narrow strip of fertile land, which gives way inland to a region of dry plains. Dotted along the coast are many small islands also occupied by the Swahili.

URBAN The Swahili are essentially seen as town dwellers although this was probably more true of the past than the present. Typically, Swahili houses were built of stone or coral and their inhabitants had a high standard of living, with plumbing, elaborate furniture, and many imported luxury goods. Town houses are now more likely to be made of *wattle-and-daub* and thatched with palm leaves. In these houses live various tradesmen, such as carpenters, leatherworkers, and builders. The Swahili no longer dominate trade in East Africa; in fact retailing is often viewed as an occupation beneath the Swahili.

RURAL Outside the towns there are strings of small villages, where farming and fishing communities live in wattle-and-daub or coral houses thatched with palm leaves. Land owning and farming are occupations that are given a relatively high status by the Swahili. Farmers

Lamu horn
This Swahili man from Lamu is blowing a brass horn called a *siwa*. Used to announce ceremonies and religious events, this siwa was made in the eighteenth century by the *lost-wax* casting method.

© DIAGRAM

Painted hands

It is customary for Swahili women to paint their hands and feet with *henna* for their wedding day, and also on other special occasions. Henna is a kind of vegetable paste that is applied on the skin in the desired patterns and left to dry. When it is removed, the skin beneath the henna has been stained a reddish brown.

Grandee's chair
Chairs such as this one were used in many Swahili royal courts from the 1300s to the 1800s. Elaborately carved in ebony and inlaid with ivory, the chair was a symbol of power and would be offered as a sign of respect to visiting notables.

mostly grow coconuts, millet, rice, sorghum, fruits, and vegetables. Fishing is also an important way of making a living for many. Women fisherfolk wade into the shallow waters of the Indian Ocean with nets to catch fish, which they carry home in baskets balanced on their heads. Fishermen sail further out to sea to the grounds where fish are plentiful.

Social organization

Unlike some African ethnic groups, the Swahili are not a completely distinct people. Having emerged over the years from the mixing of separate cultures, it can be difficult to determine which people are "true Swahili" and which are marginal peoples. The Swahili themselves give higher status to families who can claim to be "true Swahili" descended from the earliest settlers. In the past, such older and respected families were distinctive in that they controlled life in the towns; lived in the wealthiest section; were adept at Swahili verse; and dressed in the Arab-influenced fashions. Clothing today still shows Arab influence. For example, many women wear black robes, cover their heads, and veil their faces. Although, most women work as hard as the men, wealthier women stay at home and do not work. This is considered to be a symbol of status.

Culture and religion

RELIGION Swahili culture is based on their religion, which is Islam. Here, the Arab element in Swahili ancestry is paramount. The many *mosques* (Muslim houses of worship), and the ruins of many ancient ones, bear witness to the importance of religion in Swahili life.

LITERATURE The Swahili have a long history of literacy and literature. Although the Roman script is often used today, Swahili has been written for centuries in the Arabic script. There is a long tradition of elaborate poetry and written verse chronicles. The earliest known poem is the *Hamziya*, which survives in a manuscript of 1652. A group of poems in a manuscript of 1728 was probably written a century earlier. Early prose has survived in the form of a letter written in 1772. There are also many historical Swahili chronicles of particular kingdoms, for example, the *Chronicle of Pate* and the *Chronicle of Kilwa*. A Swahili history of Mombasa was translated into Arabic in 1824.

Precious comb
This comb is one of six designed for a sultan of Zanzibar by a Swahili craftsman in the nineteenth century. It is made from silver and gold and is decorative as well as functional.

Bao kiswahili
These Swahili men are playing a game called *bao kiswahili*. It is an East African version *mankala*.

© DIAGRAM

Appendix: East African languages

Africans often identify themselves by the language they speak, rather than or in addition to their ethnic origin or nationality. Language classification in Africa is complex, however; more than 1,000 languages are spoken, most of them "home" languages (native to the continent) and the rest were introduced by groups from Europe and Asia who settled in or colonized regions of Africa. Also, many Muslims learn Arabic because it is the language of the *Koran*, Islam's holy text. Swahili is widely spoken by many East Africans as a common language. As a result of this diversity, many people speak more than one language.

Among the languages introduced to Africa are English, French, Spanish, Portuguese, Afrikaans, Urdu, Hindi, Gujarati, and Malagasy. English is commonly spoken in many East African countries as it was the language of the main colonial power.

The home languages of Africa are divided into four language **families**: Niger-Kordofanian,

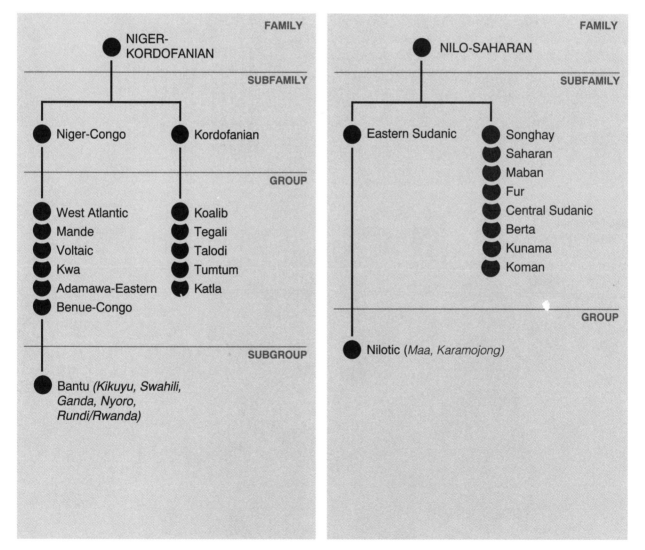

Nilo-Saharan, Afroasiatic, and Khoisan. Within these families are several **subfamilies**, many of which are also divided into **groups** and again into **subgroups** – only the relevant subgroups are shown. Some groups are themselves languages; other groups or subgroups constitute clusters of individual languages, such as the Bantu subgroup which includes the great majority of East and Southern African languages. For example, Kikuyu, the language of the Kikuyu people, and Ganda, spoken by the Ganda, are both part of the Bantu subgroup of the Benue-Congo group, which is part of the Niger-Congo subfamily of the Niger-Kordofanian language family.

Within the diagram below, the languages of the peoples profiled in this volume are printed in *italic* type. With this information, this appendix can be used to identify the subgroup, group, subfamily, and family of each language and to see how the different African languages relate to one another.

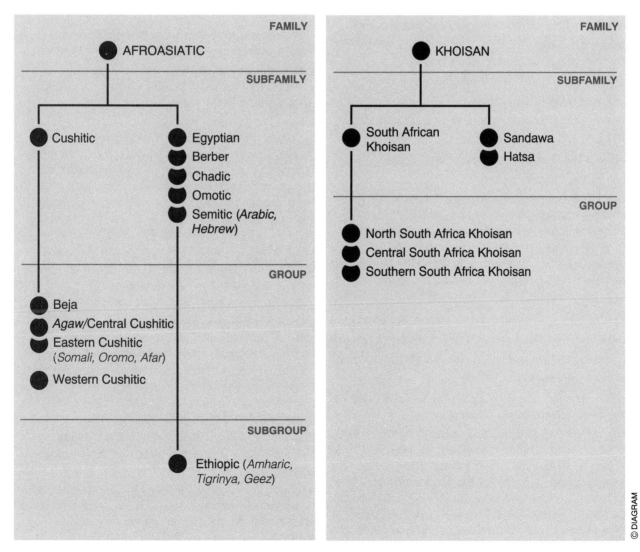

© DIAGRAM

Glossary

Bold words are cross-references to other glossary entries.

Abarusura The historic army of the Bunyoro Kingdom.

adoimara The "whites" (or lower class) in Afar society.

age-grades The various social levels in certain societies. Each person belongs to a particular age-set that moves up through the various age-grades.

age-set see age-grades

akiwor Initiation of Karamojong girls into adulthood.

Akuj The supreme god of the Karamojong religion.

aperit An overnight Karamojong festival for elders.

ari An Afar house of flexible sticks covered with mats.

asaimara The politically dominant class in Afar society.

asapan Initiation of Karamojong boys into adulthood.

askari Africans who fought in the colonial armies of German East Africa during World War I.

ayana A saint of the Oromo religion.

bakama A Bachwezi king.

bao kiswahili An East African version of mankala.

Baswezi A Nyamwezi society devoted to Swezi.

bataka The Ganda term for the head of a clan.

bebtara A Falasha religious official.

bridewealth A practice common among African people in which a marriage between a couple is sealed with a gift – often cattle, but it may be cash or other animals – from the groom to the bride's family. It is usually considered to be compensation to the bride's family for loss of a working member or a token of respect.

bugalli A Nyamwezi porridgelike dish.

bulogi Witchcraft as believed in by many Nyamwezi.

burra An Afar camp, usually comprising one or two ari.

cahen A Falasha religious official. The plural is cahenet.

cahenet see cahen

calabash A long gourdlike fruit, which – when dried and hollowed out – has many different uses.

caste A rigid class distinction generally based on birth, wealth, and occupation. The Hindu (Indian) caste system consists of four main castes, called varnas, into which a person is born. The top varna is occupied by Brahmans (religious leaders and scholars); the next consists of Kshatriyas (rulers, nobles, and warriors); then come the Vaisyas (bankers and other kinds of business people); and the lowest varna comprises the Sudras (artisans and laborers). Besides the four varnas there is a fifth category of "outcastes," called panchamas (fifths) or untouchables. Many attempts have been made to eliminate the system, and laws and modern urban life have lessened its rigidity somewhat.

ciondo A Kenyan bag made from sisal.

circumcise To carry out circumcision.

circumcision A relatively simple, if painful, procedure (removal of the foreskin) for boys but a much more serious operation (ranging form minor to severe genital mutilation) with long-lasting consequences for girls. This practice is highly controversial, however, and is opposed by many African women.

clan A group of people, usually several lineages, who claim descent from a common ancestor or ancestors.

compound An enclosure containing living quarters. Compound is often used to refer to a group of linked buildings lived in by members of the same family.

Coptic The word "Coptic" is derived from "aiguptios," the Greek word for Egyptian, which comes from an Ancient Egyptian name for Memphis. Today, the word "Coptic" has acquired many different meanings. As a noun, it is the name of an Afroasiatic language written in the Greek alphabet that is now largely extinct. Used as an adjective, Coptic can refer to the Copts (the Christian minority in Egypt); the Coptic (Christian) churches of Egypt and Ethiopia; to a historical period in Egypt's history; and to artifacts produced during that period.

dardar The head of an Afar sultanate.

deforestation The clearing of trees in a forest. The growth of urban areas has led to the intensification and extensification of agriculture: more land is needed to farm and this land is farmed more intensively leaving it little time to recover. In forest areas, this can result in a permanent loss of forest if the land is not allowed time to recover from cultivation. Deforestation causes soil deterioration, which can lead to soil erosion.

dhow A cargo ship with a raised deck at the stern (rear end) and sails, which is used along Indian Ocean coasts.

divination A common feature of many African religions, divination is practiced by diviners who use various tools (such as wooden figures, plants, bones, or seeds) to divine the spiritual cause of a specific problem such as illness, accident, or misfortune.

diviner A religious practitioner who practices **divination**.

drought Water shortage caused by a prolonged period of inadequate rainfall. Drought can have a devastating affect on the land and people who make their living from the land, in particular reducing the number of people following **nomadic** ways of life.

ekitela Subsections of Karamojong society whose members gather for festivities relating to the seasons and the harvest. Ekitela is literally the name of a reddish soil.

enkang Maasai rainy-season homes.

Epiphany A yearly festival held on January 6 in many Christian churches commemorating both the revealing of Jesus as Christ and the baptism of Jesus.

gadaa The historic Oromo democratic system.

Genna Christmas in Ethiopia.

gerber An Oromo water container made from a whole goatskin with the leg, tail, and neck openings tied.

Gikuyu According to the Kikuyu religion, the Kikuyu are descended from Gikuyu, the son of **Ngai**.

granary A building or room in which grain is stored.

groundnut A group of plants including the peanut, which is a major cash crop and food item in many African countries.

harayto A traditional top worn by rural Afar men.

henna A reddish-orange dye made from plants and used as a paint with which to decorate skin or dye hair.

hunter-gatherers People who live off food that can be hunted or collected from the wild and generally do not cultivate crops or raise livestock.

igikubge A Tutsi headdress worn by royals.

ilterekeyani The name of the most recent Maasai **age-set** to make the **age-grade** of elder.

imam A Muslim religious leader. An imam often leads the prayers at a **mosque**. The **Ismaili** Muslim subsect have an Imam as their leader.

Imana The benevolent god of the Hutu and Tutsi.

injera A pancakelike bread made from **teff**.

invertebrate Any animal without a backbone.

Ismaili A member of the Muslim subsect that has as its leader the Aga Khan. The Ismailis believe that the office of **Imam** should have gone to the descendant of Ismail (died 760) when Jafar, the sixth Imam, died in 765.

jihad An Islamic holy war against nonbelievers.

jile An Afar dagger.

kabaka A Bugandan king.

Kaikara The Nyoro harvest goddess.

kess A Falasha community priest, similar to a **rabbi**.

khanga A rectangular cloth printed with a border and a design that includes a Swahili proverb.

Kibuka The Ganda god of war, brother of **Mukasa**.

Kintu The first man and the ancestor of the Ganda.

Koran The sacred book of Islam.

kwosso A fast ball game played by the Afar.

laibon A Maasai prophet or healer.

Likube The supreme god of the Nyamwezi religion, variously referred to as Limatunda (the Creator), Limi (the Sun), or Liwelelo (the Universe).

Limatunda *see* **Likube**

Limi *see* **Likube**

lineage An extended family that shares a common ancestor. If this ancestor is male and descent is traced from father to son, the lineage is patrilineal. If the ancestor is female and descent is traced from mother to daughter, the lineage is matrilineal. Several related lineages make up a **clan**.

Liwelo *see* **Likube**

lost-wax A metal-casting method used in Africa and elsewhere for centuries. A wax model of the object is made and encased in a clay mold. When the clay mold is heated, the wax melts and molten metal is poured into its place through a hole in the mold.

Lukiko The **kabaka's** council of ministers.

maina A male Kikuyu social division that shares political power with the **mwangi**.

mankala An ancient game, played in many parts of the world, in which seeds are moved around a board.

manyatta A camp in which, for their initiation into adulthood, young Maasai men of about sixteen years of age live away from the village.

mbari A political division in Kikuyu society, literally meaning "ridge" – of which Kikuyuland has many.

mesgid A Falasha **synagogue**.

mfumu Nyamwezi **diviners**.

monoculture One-crop farming.

monsoon A seasonal wind of the Indian Ocean, or the (rainy) period during which it blows from the southwest.

Moombi In the Kikuyu religion, the wife of **Gikuyu**. According to legend she bore him nine daughters, the origin of the nine main **clans** of the Kikuyu.

moran After they have undergone **circumcision**, young Maasai men join the **age-grade** of moran, often translated as "warriors." Moran did act in the past as the Maasai army, but they mainly provide a flexible pool of labor for specific tasks such as herding.

mosque A Muslim house of worship.

Mugizi The Bachwezi god of Lake Albert.

Muhingo The Bachwezi god of war.

Mukasa The great god of the Ganda religion.

mushal *see* **shash**

mwami A Tutsi king.

mwangi A male Kikuyu social division that shares political power with the **maina**.

mwenge A beer brewed in Uganda from certain bananas.

Nambi A goddess of the Ganda religion; the daughter of the King of Heaven, and wife of **Kintu**, the first man.

Nduala The Bachwezi god of pestilence.

Ngai The all-powerful god of the Kikuyu religion. Also, the name of the supreme god of the Maasai religion.

ngikenoi Subsections of Karamojong society whose members gather for certain ceremonies. Ngikenoi literally means, "fireplaces with three stones."

ngitela Social groupings of the Karamojong people of Uganda that celebrate religious and social events together. They are determined by geography.

nomad Used to describe many, usually desert-living, peoples who follow a particular lifestyle. Nomads are "wanderers" (the word derives from "nomas," Latin for "wandering shepherd"), but they usually travel well-used paths, and their movements are dictated by the demands of trade or the needs of their herds for pasture and water.

nomadic Characteristic of, or like, **nomads** and their ways of life.

nomadism Used to describe the lifestyle of a **nomad**.

ntemi Self-governing Nyamwezi chiefdoms.

ocher A yellow or reddish-brown clay. Many people use ocher to color and style their hair.

olaiguenani A chairman of Maasai **age-grade** meetings.

omukama A king of the Bunyoro Kingdom.

orinka A Maasai ceremonial club.

orirembo A Bachwezi royal enclosure.

Orit The Falasha name for the **Torah**.

Parsee A follower of the **Zoroastrian** religion descended from Persian refugees who fled to India during the Muslim persecutions of the 600s to 700s.

Passover An eight-day Jewish festival commemorating the deliverance of the ancient Hebrews from slavery in Ancient Egypt.

pastoral Characteristic of, or like, **pastoralists** and their ways of life.

pastoralism Used to describe the lifestyle of a **pastoralist**.

pastoralist A person who raises livestock.

protectorate A state or territory that is controlled by a usually stronger nation. In particular, it is used to refer to the colonies established by Europeans in Africa. African rulers were sometimes misled, forced, or tricked into signing protectorate treaties.

pyrethrum A plant of the chrysanthemum family, or the insecticide made from the dried heads of certain varieties.

qabiil The Somali **clans**.

qalittis Female religious leaders in the Oromo religion.

qat A plant of the staff-tree family. The fresh leaf is chewed for its stimulating effects or used in tea.

quallus Hereditary Oromo religious leaders.

rabbi A Scholar and teacher of Jewish law who is qualified to decide questions of law and ritual and to perform ceremonies such as marriages.

rainforest Dense forest found in tropical areas with heavy rainfall. The trees are nearly all broadleaved evergreens, such as ironwood and mahogany. Rainforests are ecologically very rich and house a greater variety of flora and fauna than most other environments. Over the centuries, **deforestation** has removed the vast majority of rainforests in East Africa.

riika The Kikuyu name for an **age-set**.

Sabbath The Jewish holy day of rest, usually Saturday.

sanafil A traditional garment worn by the Afar; it is wrapped around the waist and tied on the right hip.

sari The main outer garment worn by Indian women, consisting of a long piece of cloth worn wrapped around the body with one end forming an ankle-length skirt and the other end draped over one shoulder.

savanna Open grasslands, often with scattered bushes or trees, characteristic of tropical Africa.

saza Historic provinces of the Bunyoro Kingdom.

scrub Dense vegetation consisting of stunted trees, bushes, and other plants. Sometimes referred to as bush.

seminomadic pastoralism A form of **pastoralism** involving the seasonal movement of livestock.

shash A black, cloth headdress traditionally worn by a married Afar woman. Also known as a mushal.

shifting cultivation A land use system in which a patch of land is cleared and cultivated until its fertility diminishes, and then abandoned until restored naturally. This type of farming has long been practiced in Africa.

shiruba A women's hairstyle common in East Africa, composed of tiny braids worn close to the scalp at the roots and loose at the ends.

Sigd A unique Falasha festival that celebrates the return of the exiles from Babylonia, led by Ezra and Nehemia.

sirata Designs on Maasai shields that indicate the **age-group** and family of the shield's owner.

sisal A strong, durable fiber made from leaves of the sisal plant; it is used to make rope, baskets, and other goods.

siwa A Swahili brass horn used to announce ceremonies and religious events.

slash and burn A method of cultivation in which a forest is cleared by cutting down and burning the trees and other vegetation for temporary agricultural use.

subsistence agriculture A type of agriculture in which all or most of the crop is consumed by the farmer and his family, leaving little or nothing for other uses.

Swezi A spirit in the Nyamwezi religion that is believed to influence people. Individuals who have been attacked or possessed by Swezi must join the **Baswezi** society in order to obtain relief from its influence.

synagogue A Jewish house of worship.

Talmud From the Hebrew for "learning," the Talmud is a collection of writings and instructions on the Jewish way of life (especially civil and religious law), based on oral teachings from the time of Moses.

teff A small, cultivated grain rich in iron and protein.

Timkat The Ethiopian name for **Epiphany**.

Torah From the Hebrew "to instruct," Torah refers to the first five books of the Old Testament regarded collectively. It can also refer to the scroll on which this is written, as used in **synagogue** services, or the whole body of traditional Jewish teaching, including Oral Law.

Towahedo The Orthodox Christian Church in Ethiopia, which has close links with the Egyptian **Coptic** Church.

tsetse fly A Bantu word that literally means "fly that kills animals." It carries tiny parasites that transmit both human and cattle diseases. The tsetse fly is widespread in East and Central Africa, especially near rivers and lakes. Its presence can make an area uninhabitable.

ubuhake A system whereby a Hutu could enter into a client relationship with a Tutsi, who would provide cattle to herd and general protection, in return for menial tasks.

ujamma A rural village in Tanzania established as part of the **villagization** policies as set out in the Arusha Declaration in 1967, after which attempts were made to reorganize Tanzanian society along socialist lines.

underemployment A situation in which although few people are totally unemployed many do not have enough work to provide for their needs. For example, this can mean that people may have a few part-time, low-paid jobs that do not fully exploit their potential.

urbanization The process of making a predominately rural area more industrialized and urban. This can involve the migration of rural people into towns.

villagization The process of restructuring rural communities into planned, often cooperatively-run and state-controlled, villages.

Waqaayo The supreme god of the Oromo religion.

wattle-and-daub A building technique using a woven latticework of sticks thickly plastered with mud or clay.

waya A togalike garment worn by Oromo men.

Zoroastrian Characteristic of, or relating to, Zoroaster or Zoroastrianism; or a follower of Zoroastrianism – the religion of the Persians before their conversion to Islam. It was founded by Zoroaster (who probably lived in about the 1200s BCE), and it includes belief in an afterlife and in the continuous struggle between good and evil. Zoroastrians pray in the presence of fire, which is considered to be a symbol of order and justice.

Index

Peoples pages and special features are printed in **bold**; *italic* page numbers refer to illustrations, captions, or maps.

A

Abatembuzi people 84
Adowa, Battle of *18*
Afar language 33, *105*
Afar people **32–35**
  distribution of 24
Afar religion 35
Afar sultanates 35
Afroasiatic languages 105, *105*
Aga Khan 47
Agaw language 50, *105*
Agriculture 30, 40, 47, 54, 56,
  81, 82, 86
  see also Farming
Ali, Ras 89
Amhara people **38–41**, **89**, **91**, **92**
  distribution of 24
Amharic language 39, 50, *105*
Amharic script 39, *40*
Amin Dada, Idi *19*, 46, 63, 86
Arab people *17*, 27, 29, 38, 94, 98,
  99, *99*, 100, 102
Arabic language 29, 96, *96*, 100,
  104, *105*
Area of countries 6
Ark of the Covenant 38
Arusha Declaration 80, 81
Arusha Maasai people 70, 71
Arusi Oromo people 88
Asians, East African 29, **44–47**
  distribution of 25
Australopithecines *36*, 36, 37, *37*
Axumite Kingdom *23*, 27, 38, 39, 49
  statue *16*

B

Babito dynasty 84, 85
Babito people 85, 87
Bachwezi dynasty 84, 87, *87*
Baganda *see* Ganda people
Bahima people 78, 87
Bahutu *see* Hutu people
Bairu people 87
Bantu peoples 26, 52, 98
Banyoro *see* Nyoro people
Bararetta Oromo people 88
Barre, Muhammad Siad 95
Basese Ganda people 52, 53
Basketwork *58*, *79*
Beadwork *69*, *73*
Begemder, Kingdom of 89
Beta Israel *see* Falasha people

Bokora Karamojong people 62
Borana Oromo people 88, *93*
Bridewealth 60, 61, 65
Buganda Kingdom 27, *53*, *54*, *55*, 85
Buildings *17*, 34, *35*, *41*, *42*, *45*, *49*,
  50, 50, *51*, *54*, *64*, 73, *82*, *90*, *91*, 97
Bunyoro Kingdom 27, 53, 86
Bunyoro-Kitara Empire 84, *85*, *87*
Burundi
  area, GNP, population 6
  civil war 6, *20*, 59, *61*
  colonialism and independence 21
  distribution of peoples *24*
  location on map *5*, *7*

C

Camels *33*, 72, 73, *79*, 90, *95*, *96*
Cash crops 6, 30, 54, **56–57**, 68, 86
Cattle 33, 60, 62, 63, 64, 65, 70, 71,
  72, *72*, 74, *75*, 84, 86, 96
Christianity 30, 49, **42–43**
  Amhara people 39, 41
  Axumite Kingdom 39, 42
  Ganda people 55
  Hutu people 61
  Kikuyu people 69
  Nyamwezi people 83
  Nyoro people 87
  Oromo people 91
  Tutsi people 61
Chronologies
  events to 1884 16–17
  events 1886–1987 18–19
  events 1988 – present day 20–21
Circumcision 35, 41, 51, 69, 74
Climate 10–11
Clothing *33*, *34*, 35, *47*, *60*, *61*,
  61, *68*, *74*, 74, *81*, *83*, 90, 102
Coastal lowlands 9, *83*
Coffee 56, *57*
Colonialism *17*, 27, 39, 45, 47, 53,
  63, 66–67, 68, 72, 81, 82, 85, 95
  dates of occupation and
  independence 21
Comoros Is 101
Conservation 76, 77, 78
Coptic Christianity 41, 43
Crafts 73, *79*, 91, *100*
Crosses *39*, *43*
Cushitic peoples 26, 38, 88, 94, 98

D

Danakil *see* Afar people
Dancing 75, *83*
Darwin, Charles 36
Defenses *17*, *87*

Deforestation 13, 31
Deserts 28
  vegetation 12
  wildlife 14
Divination 83
Division of labor 40–41, 64, 90
Djibouti
  area, GNP, population 6
  colonialism and independence 21
  distribution of peoples *24*
  location on map *5*, *7*
Dodoth Karamojong people 62

E

Early humans 26, **36–37**
East Africa
  introduction 26–31
  today 6–7
East African Indian National
  Congress 45
Eastern Highlands 8
Eritrea
  area, GNP, population 6
  colonialism and independence 21
  distribution of peoples *24*
  liberation from Ethiopia *20*, 21, 39, 89
  location on map *5*, *7*
Eritrean Popular Liberation
  Front (EPLF), insignia *20*
Esther, Queen 49
Ethiopia
  area, GNP, population 6
  civil war 39, 40, 89
  distribution of peoples *24–25*
  location on map *5*, *7*
Ethiopian Empire 27
Ethnic groups
  definition 5
  distribution 24–25
  population figures 29
Ezana, King 39

F

Falasha people **48–51**
  distribution of 24
Farming 6, 30, 50, 56, 63, 68, 82,
  90, 96, 97, 101
  see also Agriculture
Fasilida, King *49*
Figurines *18*, *81*, *82*
Fishing 101, 102
Forests 28
  deforestation 31
  vegetation 13
Fossils 36, *36*
Furniture 65, *83*, *102*

G

Gafabusa, Sir Tito Winyi *86*
Gafabusa Iguru, Solomon 86
Galagansa Nyamwezi people 80
Galla *see* Oromo people
Game reserves 77
Ganda language 54, *104*
Ganda people 27, **52–55**
  distribution of 25
Ganda religion 55
Geez language 22, 39, *42, 51, 105*
Geography of East Africa 28
  climate 10–11
  East Africa today 6–7
  land 8–9
  vegetation 12–13
  wildlife 14–15
George, Saint *40*
Gikuyu *see* Kikuyu people
GNP 6
Gujarati language 46, 100, 104

H

Ha chiefdom 80
Hadza people 26
Haile Selassie I, Emperor *19*, 27, *39*, 89
Hairstyles *35, 64, 71, 92,* **92–93**, *93*
Hebrew language 50, 51, *105*
Henna *102*
Hinduism *45,* 47
History of East Africa
  chronologies 16–21
  overview 27
  pictorial 22–23
Hominids **36–37**
Horn of Africa 9, 10, 12, 28, *93*
Hunting, big-game 72, *76*
Hutu people 6, **58–61**
  distribution of 25

I

Independence, dates of 21
Industry 73, 86
Ishmaili Muslims 47
Islam 30, 42
  Afar people 35
  Amhara people 39
  East African Asians 47
  Ganda people 55
  Nyamwezi people 83
  Nyoro people 87
  Oromo people 91
  Somali people 94–95, 97
  Swahili people 103
Israel, and Falasha people 48, 49
Itu Oromo people 88

J

Jews, Falasha people **48–51**
Jie Karamojong people 62
Judaism 48, 49, 50, 51
Judith, Queen 49

K

Kabalega 85
Kaboyo Omuhanwa 85
Karamojong language 63, *104*
Karamojong people 26, **62–65**, *93*
  distribution of 24
Karamojong religion 65
Kassa 89
Kenya *57*
  area, GNP, population 6
  colonialism and independence 21
  distribution of peoples *24*
  location on map *5, 7*
  tourism 78, *78*
Kenya African National Union
  (KANU) 67
Kenyatta, Jomo *21*, 67
Khanga cloth *99*
Khoisan languages 105, *105*
Kikuyu language 68, *104*, 105
Kikuyu people 27, **66–69**
  distribution of 25
Kikuyu religion 69
Kimeu, Kimoya 37
Kinyarwanda *see* Rwanda language
Kirundi *see* Rundi language
Kiswahili *see* Swahili language
Koran 29, 104
Kwosso game *34*
Kyembame Nyamutukura III 85

L

Laikipiak Maasai people 71
Lakes, wildlife 14
Lalibela *42,* 42–43
Land 8–9
Languages 29–30, 47, 55, 65, 61, 69, 75, 83, 87, 91, **104–105**
Leakey family 37
Lifestyles 30
"Lucy" hominid 36, *37*
Luganda *see* Ganda language
Luzira Head *54*
Lwo peoples 85, 87

M

Maa language 71, *104*
Maasai language *see* Maa language
Maasai people 26, **70–75**, *79, 93*
  and wildlife 76, 77, 79
  distribution of 25

hairstyles *93*
  see also Moran
Maasai religion 75
Macha Oromo people 88
Malawi
  area, GNP, population 6
  colonialism and independence 21
  distribution of peoples *24*
  location on map *5, 7*
Mankala game *100, 103*
Maria Theresa dollars 89, *91*
Mark, Saint 42
Marriage 35, 41, 60–61, 65, 97
  see also Bridewealth
Matheniko Karamojong people 62
Mau Mau rebellion *18, 67, 78*
Mbatiany 71
Menelik I 38, 48
Menelik II 89
Micombero, Michel 58
Mining 30
Mirambo 81
Moi, Daniel arap 67
Monsoons *17,* 28
Moran *71, 74, 75, 93*
Mosques *103*
Mountains 9, 10, 28, *69,* 70
  vegetation 12, 13
  wildlife 14
Mpuga Rukidi 85
Muhammad, Prophet 95
Muhammad Siad Barre 95
Muslims *see* Islam, Ismaili Muslims
Music *55, 83, 87, 101*
Mutesa I *53,* 54
Mutesa II 54, *55*
Mwambusta IV 58

N

National parks 15, *77*
Ngeneo, Bernard 37
Ngoni chiefdom 80
Niger-Kordofanian languages *104,* 104–105
Nilo-Saharan languages *104,* 105
Nilotic peoples 26, 70
Nomadic pastoralism 30, 33, 66, 71, 96, 97, *97*
Nomadism 32, 34
Ntemi chiefs *81*
Nyamwezi language 81
Nyamwezi people 27, **80–83**, *93*
  distribution of 25
Nyamwezi religion 83
Nyerere, Julius *21,* 81
Nyoro language 86, *104*
Nyoro people 27, **84–87**

Index

distribution of 25
Nyoro religion 87

O

Obote, Milton 86
Oldowan Culture 37
Olduvai Gorge *37*, 37
Omani Arabs 99, *99*
Omukama *85*, 85, *86*
Orit (Torah) 51, *51*
Oromo language 89, *105*
Oromo people 26, **88–91**, 95
  distribution of 24–25

P

Parsees 47
Pastoral nomadism *see* Nomadic
  pastoralism
Pastoralism 33, 66, 72, 87, 89
Peoples of East Africa
  distribution 24–25
  introduction 26–31
  today 6–7, 29, 30
Persians 27, 29, 47, 94, 98, 99
Petroleum 87
Pian Karamojong people 62
Population 6
  density 7
  ethnic groups 29
  major cities 7
Pottery *50*, *53*, *54*, *86*
Punjabi language 46

R

Railroads 6
  East African Railway 45
  "Lunatic Line" *45*, *46*
Rainfall 10–11
Rainforests 13, 28
Randili people 88
Religions 29–30, 47, 55, 65,
  61, 69, 75, 83, 87, 91
  see also Christianity, Islam, Judaism
Rift Valley, Great 8, 28, *37*, *67*, 70
Rivers, wildlife 15
Roads, major 6
Ruanda-Urundi Kingdom 58
Rundi language 59, *104*
Rwabudongo 85
Rwanda
  area, GNP, population 6
  civil war 6, 59, *61*
  colonialism and independence 21
  distribution of peoples *24*
  location on map *5*, *7*
Rwanda language 59, *104*

S

Salt 34, *35*, *41*, 87
Samburu Maasai people 70, 72,
  73, *79*, *93*
Sandawe people 26
Sarsa Dengal, Emperor 49
Savannas 28
  vegetation 12
  wildlife 14
Sea, wildlife 15
Semideserts 28
  vegetation 12
  wildlife 14
Seychelles
  area, GNP, population 6
  colonialism and independence 21
  location on map *5*, *7*
  tourism 79
Seyyid Said, Sultan 99
Sheba, Queen of 38, 48
Sheikh Hussein *91*
Shields *68*, *71*, *72*
Shirazi dynasty 98
Shore, wildlife 14
Sikhism *46*, 47
Slash and burn 30
Slave trade *17*, 27, 100
Solomon, King 38, 48
Solomon Gafabusa Iguru 86
Solomonic dynasty 39, 48
Somali language 96, *105*
Somali people **94–97**
  distribution of 24
Somalia
  area, GNP, population 6
  civil war 6, *20*, 95
  colonialism and independence 21
  distribution of peoples *24–25*
  location on map *5*, *7*
Subsistence agriculture 30
Susneyos, Emperor 49
Swahili language 29, 46, 81,
  100–101, 104, *104*
Swahili people *16*, 29, **98–103**
  distribution of 25

T

Taitu, Queen 89
Tanzania
  area, GNP, population 6
  colonialism and independence 21
  distribution of peoples *24*
  location on map *5*, *7*
  tourism 78–79
Tea 56–57, *57*
Temperature 10–11

Temples
  Hindu *45*
  Sikh *46*
Tewodros (Theodore) II, Emperor 89
Tigrinya language 50, *105*
Tombs
  Mutesa I *54*
  Oromo *91*
Toro Kingdom 27, 85
Tourism 6, 31, 73, **76–79**
Towahedo Christian Church 41
Trade *17*, 27, 28, 30, 31, 44,
  47, 68, 81, 82, 98, 99
Tulama Oromo people 88
Turkana people 62
Tutsi people 6, **58–61**
  distribution of 25
Twa people 58, 61

U

Uganda
  area, GNP, population 6
  civil war 6, 86
  colonialism and independence 21
  distribution of peoples *24*
  location on map *5*, *7*
  tourism 78
Ujamaas 81
Urbanization 31
Urdu language 100, 104

V

Vegetation 12–13
Villagization 72, 81

W

Walega Oromo people 88
Wamara, Bakama 84
Wanyamwezi *see* Nyamwezi people
Watutsi *see* Tutsi people
Wildlife 14–15, 72, *76–79*, 96
Winds 10
Wollo Oromo people 88
World Bank 72
Writing
  Amharic script 39, *40*

Y

Yekuno Amlak, King 39

Z

Zagwe dynasty 42, 49
Zanzibar Sultanate 99–100
  colonialism and independence 21
  slave market *17*, 27, 100
Zinza chiefdom 80
Zoroastrians 47